In the moonlight, the angular planes in his face made him look even more appealing. "Please, Anne Marie, give me a chance. I know you must think I don't deserve it..."

She saw a boyish hopefulness in his eyes that touched her heart. She turned her face up to his.

His lips touched hers softly, almost reverently. She slipped her hands around his neck, and her fingers moved through his hair just as she'd dreamed those summers when she was a girl.

Suddenly, reason reasserted itself, and she stepped back. "No more..."

"You're right," he agreed firmly.

What was wrong with her? Last night she'd run from Alex's advances and now she was returning Jon's kiss. What sort of a woman was she?

Jon looked at the night sky. "I can't say I'm sorry, but it was unplanned, no matter what you might think. Unplanned but wonderful."

Palisades.
Pure Romance.

Fiction that features credible characters and entertaining plot lines, while continuing to uphold strong Christian values. From high adventure to tender stories of the heart, each Palisades Romance is an undiluted story of love, from beginning to end!

A PALISADES CONTEMPORARY ROMANCE

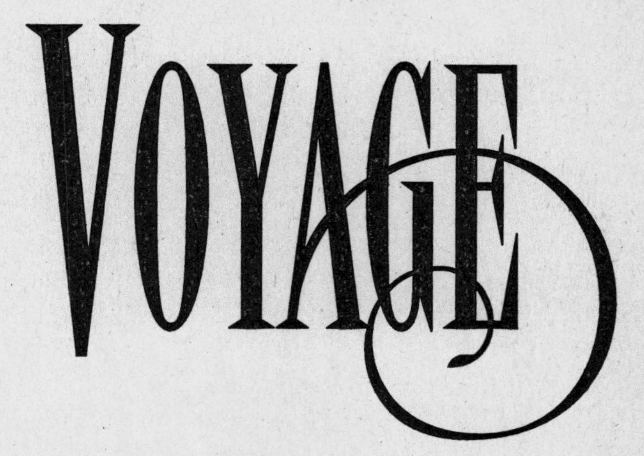

ELAINE L. SCHULTE

This is a work of fiction. The characters, incidents, and dialogues are products of the author's imagination and are not to be construed as real. Any resemblance to actual events or persons, living or dead, is entirely coincidental.

VOYAGE
published by Palisades
a part of the Questar publishing family

International Standard Book Number: 1-57673-011-5

Cover illustration by George Angelini
Cover designed by David Carlson and
Mona Weir-Daly
Edited by Diane Noble

Printed in the United States of America

Scripture quotations are from:

The King James Version (KJV)

For information:
QUESTAR PUBLISHERS, INC.
POST OFFICE BOX 1720
SISTERS, OREGON 97759

96 97 98 99 00 01 02 03 — 10 9 8 7 6 5 4 3 2 1

Dedication

to Gayle Gillies, the arranger,

and to Charles and Rachel Dierenfield and

all of those in the Rancho Santa Fe Village Church group

who traveled with us.

Enter his gates with thanksgiving and his courts with praise...

PSALMS 100:4 (NIV)

Prologue

Anne Marie Gardene smoothed her blue denim skirt nervously as she rode with her parents to the Lincoln, Nebraska airport. Her family knew little about the Greek exchange student they were to pick up, but enough to make him more interesting than most boys her age.

Her father, a French professor, drove. "A wonderful opportunity," he remarked in his professorial tone. "How many families can host the heir to a world-renowned Greek shipping line?"

"Very few," her mother agreed, "but it all happened so quickly. I don't know. With a young teenage girl in the house..."

Anne Marie stiffened her shoulders. Maybe she was young, but it didn't mean that she didn't understand a lot. As for their exchange student, Alexander Andropoulos would live with them for six months to perfect his English. He was older—seventeen years old—and would attend Harvard in the fall to major in business.

At the airport, they hurried to his gate and Anne Marie turned to the incoming passengers. There he was! More handsome than his photo: angular face with a straight nose, narrow lips, a dimple in his chin, brown eyes with long lashes, and smooth, raven-black hair.

As Anne Marie stepped forward with her parents, Alex beamed. "Professor Gardene?" His dark eyes were lively.

"Yes," her father replied with pleasure. Few people used the title, and at sixty, he was of what he called "the old school" about titles. "Yes, I'm Professor Gardene."

"I am Alex Andropoulos," he said with an accent, then shook hands heartily with her father.

Her father sounded less formal than usual as he introduced them. "This is Mrs. Gardene and our daughter, Anne Marie."

Anne Marie was startled as Alex extended his firm hand, his gaze meeting hers with interest. "A pleasure to meet you, Anne Marie."

"Thank you," she managed as she let him shake her hand.

"You're the age of my little sister, Anna," he remarked, flashing his white smile at her. "Anna—Anne Marie. Very similar."

She returned his smile, even though she disliked being compared to his little sister.

"I have three married sisters," he added, "and of course, Anna." His low voice took on pride mingled with resignation. "I'm the son, the only son."

"That would be important in your family," Anne Marie's father observed.

"Yes, very important."

At home, Alex settled into the Gardene guest room, brightening the house with his enthusiasm and curiosity about life in the United States. It seemed to Anne Marie that his presence brought the sun's rays closer to earth.

Before long she began to wonder if she was falling in love

with him. She had never felt this way before. But maybe it wasn't so strange, because plenty of high school girls chased after Alex. When he left for a date, she'd watch him from her upstairs bedroom window, imagining him smiling at the girl, then slipping his arms around her—imagining until her heart ached. Once he glanced back at her window so abruptly she was caught.

The months passed. As the time neared for his return to Greece for the summer, Anne Marie's heart twisted with anguish. She'd miss his uplifted dark brow when he smiled, his rueful shrugs, his hearty Greek laughter, his dramatic gestures as he spoke with that wonderful accent.

The Monday afternoon of his last week, she heard him downstairs opening kitchen cabinets. She hurried quietly down the steps and stood watching as he took food from the refrigerator, then carried it to the oak breakfast table.

I should fix him in my memory forever, she thought. Dark hair turning up at the nape of his neck. His chiseled face. The cleft in his chin.

He glanced up. "I am going to miss you, Anne Marie," he said as if he'd been aware of her presence.

"Oh, Alex..." Her throat caught, and she felt mesmerized by his luminous eyes.

He laughed, his expression affectionate. "You're so like my little sister."

Tears welled in her eyes. "I don't want to be like a sister to you. I'm growing up..." She faltered.

He stepped closer.

She lifted her gaze to his dark eyes.

"I know you are," he murmured. His expression held the warmth of the sunlight streaming through the kitchen window. His face neared hers, and she caught her breath, awaiting her first kiss.

But quite suddenly a car door slammed outside the kitchen window, and they pulled apart guiltily.

Alex peered through the sheer white curtains over the kitchen sink. "Your mother!"

Silence filled the space around them in the kitchen. "Tonight," he finally whispered. "We can walk after dinner." He paused. "But for now...I'll run and bring in the groceries."

She nodded. Her sandals felt stuck to the floor as she watched him hurry to the car.

Her mother stepped through the kitchen door, a curious expression on her face. "Are you all right?"

"Yes," Anne Marie answered, swallowing hard. "Yes, I'm fine."

Her mother frowned, and Anne Marie bolted out the door. "I'll help unload the car."

Passing Alex as she headed for the garage, he winked over the armload of groceries.

A movement at the kitchen window caught her attention. Her mother peered at them between the curtains. Turning, Anne Marie rushed to the car's open trunk and lifted out two more bags.

Later, as she helped put the food away, her mother asked, "Is something wrong, dear? You seem so far away."

Blood rushed to her face again. "I...I don't know."

At dinner, her father remarked, "We're going to miss you, Alex. It's been like having a son for a while."

"Thank you, sir," Alex answered. "You have all been very good to me. I couldn't have asked for a finer host family."

Anne Marie watched her father's smile. He enjoyed being called *sir* as much as he liked being called *professor,* but this time his smile was somehow different. "We especially appreciate the respectful way in which you've treated Anne Marie," her father said in a careful tone.

Anne Marie's heart constricted as her father continued. "Anne Marie has never had a brother or been around young men much, so the example you've set will be an important one for her life—for her impression of men." Her father spoke on and on about how some young men might violate the hospitality in a home where there was a young lady.

She flushed in embarrassment, knowing that she and Alex would not go for a moonlit walk after all. And it was her own fault for giving her feelings away.

"I know you'll miss Alex, too, Anne Marie," her father said. He looked at her, awaiting her reaction.

The word came out in a whisper. "Yes."

"I'm going to miss all of you," Alex said, but his gaze locked on hers.

That night she lay in bed, thinking about the day's events. She thought of her father's words and was suddenly struck by his solemn manner. *What if his heart is bothering him again?* she thought with sudden terror. His health was precarious. What if her actions caused another heart attack? Nothing—not even Alex—was worth that risk.

She didn't meet Alex again until right before he left. One morning just before math class, she opened her book and found a folded sheet of Alex's special graph paper. She opened the paper with trembling fingers. *Meet me at the public library after school. Reference room.*

After school, she nearly ran the five blocks to the library. Stepping into the reference room, she drew in a deep breath to calm her pounding heart. She forced herself to walk slowly among the tables to the ceiling-high shelves of books. Had he remembered her favorite table, the one hidden near the window, the one she'd shown to him the first week he'd been in Lincoln?

As she turned the corner, she saw him there, seated at her special table. The afternoon sun slanted through the quivering trees by the window, dappling light all around him.

He looked up over a book, then immediately rose to his feet. "I didn't know if you would come." His accent was more enchanting than ever.

The sun sparkled all around them as if they were encircled in a golden shower of light. When they finally sat down, he held her hands in his across the small table and whispered, "Oh...Anne Marie. How I will miss you. I shouldn't have waited so long, but I worried about your father."

For an instant, fear intruded. "Will I ever see you again?" She felt like crying.

"Of course, my little Anne Marie. Someday..."

She knew what he meant. He was her first love, and someday she hoped they would be together forever and ever.

After he flew to Greece, Alex wrote a gracious letter, thanking them all for his stay. Then there'd been a postcard of the Acropolis in Athens, again for all of them. Anne Marie's loneliness turned into heartache when no more letters arrived all summer. Nearly every week she went to the library, trying to relive the wonder of their last moments alone.

Someday, he'd said. *Someday...*

In December, he sent a Christmas card from Harvard, then a postcard. And finally, nothing at all.

But she never forgot the shimmering moments spent with her first love in their bower of sunshine.

Two summers later, Anne Marie's father died of the heart attack she had feared, and her mother took a full-time position at the university. Heartbroken, and feeling like she'd lost all that was near and dear to her, Anne Marie flew to California to stay with Aunt Sylvia in Santa Rosita, who slowly helped her work through her grief.

Early on a July morning she heard a young man talking and laughing out on the patio with Aunt Sylvia. "Where is this Anne Marie?" His low voice lingered on her name, making it sound beautiful. Could it be Jon, the young man her aunt had told her about?

Leaves rustled faintly in the breeze and birds twittered from the trees. It seemed that time hung suspended in the morning light as she stepped forward through the open french doors toward him.

At first he seemed unaware of her presence as he stood under the sprawling California pepper tree with her aunt. He wore white—a T-shirt and tennis shorts—and his dark brown hair glowed with reddish highlights where the sun shimmered through the willowy branches of the tree. Aunt Sylvia had said that he was a fine and godly young man. But she hadn't mentioned how handsome he was.

Quite suddenly, he looked at her with his amazingly blue eyes.

"Hi," she barely managed. "I'm Anne Marie."

"Hi," he responded with a friendly smile.

"This is Jon," her aunt said. "Actually Jonathan Barnett. He's about to graduate from law school."

"I'm a senior in high school," Anne Marie jabbered, then wished she'd held her tongue.

"You two dears sit down and get acquainted," Aunt Sylvia suggested. "Let me carry out the breakfast things. I've made caramel cream for the waffles."

"Let me help," Jon said.

"Me, too," Anne Marie added, finding it difficult to keep her gaze off him.

"I won't hear of it," her aunt told them, then smiled and hurried inside.

Anne Marie sat down at the glass-topped patio table with him, feeling something special awaken inside her. She scarcely touched the waffles; instead she memorized the contours of Jon's high forehead, the azure shade of his eyes, his fine high cheekbones.

Delighted by Anne Marie's interest in Jon, her aunt maneuvered them into group outings together: a day across the Mexican border in Tijuana, a neighborhood barbecue, beach parties. Anne Marie saw him almost daily, but he treated her as a younger sister, too—someone to take fishing and to the beach, someone to help him wash his red sports car before he went out on *real* dates.

Still, he helped her forget her father's death and eased the ache of loneliness. And he helped her to forget about Alex Andropoulos.

One hot July morning while she and Jon fished from a rowboat on the nearby lake, she lifted her heavy blond hair from the back of her perspiring neck, hoping to catch a breeze.

Jon gazed at her strangely and set aside his fishing pole. "Would you like for me to braid your hair? It might be cooler." He smiled, and in the blinding sunshine, his white teeth seemed a flash of light against his tan.

Anne Marie was surprised by his suggestion. "You?" Then she laughed softly. The brilliance of the sunlight, the loveliness of the still lake and the surrounding hills—even his intense expression entranced her. She smiled and nodded. "Okay. It's too hot today for long hair anyhow."

She turned her back to him, closing her eyes at the pleasure of feeling his hands combing through her hair. "It's beautiful, Anne Marie," he murmured as he worked. "Reminds me of a halo." His usually calm voice held a tremor of uncertainty.

When he finished, they sat in the bobbing boat, and his eyes met hers. She wondered if he was thinking of kissing her. But without another word, he took up his fishing pole.

She let out a disappointed breath. Jon was too much older and too much of a gentleman to kiss her, she decided. Besides, she'd probably read too much into his braiding her hair.

When Anne Marie graduated from high school the following spring, Jon was already a practicing attorney. The years between them seemed an insurmountable difference; nonetheless, when Aunt Sylvia phoned and mentioned his engagement, a stab of pain twisted in Anne Marie's heart.

For years she remembered him on the patio that first summer morning under the pepper tree, his blue-eyed gaze turning to her. But especially, she remembered the sunlit moments in the rowboat when he'd braided her hair.

Her college and kindergarten teaching years passed by almost uneventfully, then her mother suddenly died in a freeway accident. If that weren't heartbreaking enough, only months later Anne Marie was summoned to the bedside of her dying Aunt Sylvia.

Frail and weak, she looked up at her niece from the hospital bed. She smiled softly and reached for Anne Marie's hand. "If I can't go on the cruise, I want you to use my ticket." Her eyes were dim as if an inner light were fading. "I've told everyone who needs to know. And Jonathan has the codicil."

"You mustn't talk like that!" Anne Marie protested. "You'll be fine. I know it."

Since Anne Marie's mother had died, her aunt had been the one person left on earth who truly loved her. And now that she thought of it, the only person left on earth whom she truly loved, too.

"Don't be frightened, dear," Aunt Sylvia replied. "I'm eager for heaven."

"No! I don't want to hear it! Aunt Sylvia, I love you too much to let you go!"

Her aunt's expression softened as she spoke. "It's my prayer that you'll come to understand how much God loves you—that his love is forgiving, constant, eternal. He's always loving you, even when your back is turned to him. He cares about every detail of your life."

"I can't bear to talk about it!" Anne Marie cried.

Her aunt's eye lids drifted closed and sadness filled her voice. "I can understand your heartache. It must seem to you that everyone has abandoned you, but he hasn't. The Lord hasn't."

No one understands! Anne Marie thought angrily. *No one! Least of all God.*

"Please, please don't go!" Her voice was a ragged whisper. "Aunt Sylvia, I love you!"

"Both of our lives are in the Lord's hands—where they belong," her aunt murmured. "Just remember God cares deeply about you, Anne Marie."

Her aunt slipped into a coma. Later that night, she simply stopped breathing.

Grief was only part of the problem, Anne Marie thought. Every person she loved most dearly had left her. Her parents had died. Alex had broken off his communication. Jon had become engaged to another. And now Aunt Sylvia had left her, too.

Never in her life had she felt such loss, such utter abandonment.

Never in her life had she felt so alone.

CHAPTER

One

Something wonderful is happening, Anne Marie thought as she blinked awake on the darkened airplane. She sat up groggily before the excitement surged through her again. *She was on her way to a Mediterranean cruise!* It seemed incredible because she rarely traveled, but as she awakened more fully, she felt vague misgivings about being on a Holy Land pilgrimage.

Oh, to stand up and stretch!

The Los Angeles to London leg of the flight had been tiring enough, and there'd been a three-hour layover in London before their group boarded this flight to Athens.

She glanced at Jon Barnett, who dozed quietly beside her, and knew he was the cause of some of her apprehensions. Right now, he had her trapped in the window seat, and she suspected he'd been partially responsible for trapping her into this trip, as well.

In any event, it was downright peculiar to be sitting beside him. He looked older than he had that summer they'd met, but then she was eight years older, too. Fortunately her stage of adolescent infatuation with him had ended.

Nonetheless, she couldn't help taking a good look at him.

Rangy, slightly dark, and attractive in a patrician manner... Actually he'd be quite handsome if she weren't so furious with him.

The constant roar of the plane's engines muffled the sound as she unzipped her huge navy blue handbag and rummaged in it for the shell-shaped gold compact that had once been Aunt Sylvia's. Her fingers felt the cosmetic pouch, but no compact. Most likely, it was buried under her wadded nylon raincoat.

At any rate, even if she found the mirror, she'd see only bits of her oval face in it. Her slightly upturned nose with its dusting of freckles. Her wisps of honey blond hair curling around her face, having escaped the sleek chignon at the nape of her neck.

Hair like a halo, Jon had called it that golden morning. She suddenly wondered if he'd ever had the chance to braid his late fiancée's hair before she died in that tragic accident.

She glanced into her handbag, wanting to concentrate on the exciting fax from Athens instead. No, she couldn't read it again now. Pulling the handbag's drawstring, she gave up the search for the compact as well.

"Nice to open my eyes and find a beautiful young woman in the seat beside me," Jon murmured. His blue eyes peered from under dark lashes. A mischievous smile tugged at his lips.

"I thought you were asleep."

"I *was* asleep," Jon responded, still smiling. He added, "I'm serious about what I said. Looking at you from this angle, you are lovely. Actually, from any angle."

Hmmph! She pushed the handbag under the seat.

Eight years ago his words and smile might have turned her weak-kneed, she thought. She brushed non-existent lint from the ribbed cuff of her lapis-blue pantsuit. As for her being beautiful, her father had once said she had "a country girl's face with eyes as blue as Nebraska cornflowers."

Wholesome, he'd meant.

Now he'd probably consider her too thin for her five feet six inches. Her one show of sophistication was the tight chignon Aunt Sylvia's hairdresser claimed would be neat for travel. It did make her look twenty-three years old, though last year's kindergartners would scarcely recognize their teacher without her yellow curls.

"I can see that compliments will get me nowhere," Jon said as he sat up stiffly. "Where are we?"

Tugging up the white plastic window shade, Anne Marie was surprised to see daylight. Craggy foothills and snow-peaked mountains jutted sharply from the grayness of the earth, and here and there sunshine shimmered on lakes, turning them into silvery mirrors. "I don't know."

"Too bad this plane doesn't have a position map on the screen." He unfastened his seatbelt and leaned slightly across her to glance out the window, the musky fragrance of his aftershave unnerving her. "The Swiss Alps, or maybe Italy's Dolomites."

"I suppose you'd know," she replied, trying to achieve a level tone.

"Do I detect a hint of resentment?"

She decided not to answer.

Aunt Sylvia had loved him as though he were her own child, even financing part of his education. Despite the fact that he specialized in international business law, she'd appointed him to be her estate attorney. Then two months ago, he hadn't even flown home from Europe for the services. It was outrageous and disloyal, at the very least.

"We'll be flying over Italy and then to Athens," Jon remarked, still gazing out past her.

"So the pilot told us," she responded.

"My, you are testy this morning." He settled back into his

seat again. "Is this the sweet Anne Marie I remember?"

She turned, staring blindly out the window. She should be cheery like Aunt Sylvia, even though her aunt had sometimes seemed too forgiving. Not to mention too devoted to matchmaking.

That first summer, despite the difference in their ages, Aunt Sylvia had been all too interested in bringing off a romance between them.

Even this trip seemed part of her intrigue. Anne Marie could either take this Mediterranean cruise with her aunt's church group or donate the ticket to someone who would be chosen by Jon Barnett, according to the last-minute codicil to the will.

"Isn't that your Aunt Sylvia's charm bracelet you're wearing?"

"Yes. Yes, it is."

"She always added charms to it when she traveled."

Anne Marie fingered the tiny gold charms: a Jerusalem cross from Israel; a leaning tower of Pisa; the Venetian gondola; a Dutch windmill; the Eiffel Tower; an English castle…

"It always intrigued me," Jon said. "I suppose the charms held the mystique of faraway places."

"It's always intrigued me, too," she admitted without quite looking at him.

After an uneasy silence, he spoke as if he wanted to keep their conversation on safe ground. "I suppose you have a shopping mission."

"Only for inexpensive mementos for my kindergartners, and in Crete, a Minoan-style fresco for a school teacher friend. I'm not one of those shop-till-you-droppers, if that's what you're implying. Besides, it seems that attorneys have mishandled my funds."

He shot a glance at her, took a deep breath, and hunkered down in the seat. "May as well sleep."

"May as well," she responded angrily.

After a long time, she glanced at him again.

He was apparently asleep this time, his tall frame jammed into the middle seat. He wore a well-tailored navy blue blazer, light gray slacks, and a pale blue shirt, open at the collar, exposing his thick neck. Dark brown hair fell rakishly over his forehead, and black lashes curled near his high cheek bones. His beard had grown out slightly, an arresting change from his usual dignified appearance. In her teen years she'd have been ecstatic to have him so close, but now she knew enough to resist the subtle intimacy of waking up beside him on a plane.

Strange that the two loves in her life had come during her teen summers: Alex Andropoulos and Jon Barnett. After Alex and Jon, the procession of high school boys and young college men had been uninspiring. Strange, too, that she was sitting on this plane with Jon—and had the exciting fax from Alex in her handbag.

Jon's low voice jolted her thoughts. "I don't like you to be so irritated with me. Let's try to clear the air."

"I thought you were asleep again," she replied.

"I tried," he admitted with an ironic smile at her.

She looked away. It was senseless to rake up the problems his absence had caused after her aunt's death. The elderly attorney substituted by the law firm had been too busy to spend enough time on her aunt's complex affairs, many of which awaited Anne Marie's return.

"I hope you're not worrying about terrorism."

She blinked in astonishment. "To be perfectly honest, I haven't given it much thought. I suppose I'm like all tourists, thinking the tourist stops are safe; that fighting and terrorists have nothing to do with me."

"I see. I thought the trouble at the airport in New York might have upset you."

"I'm just glad airport security is tight," she replied.

The *trouble,* as he'd termed the terrifying incident, was a bomb threat that led to the removal of every piece of luggage from the plane. The passengers had exited calmly as the plane was searched. Anne Marie had half-expected the plane to explode right there.

"Then I suppose your frosty glances are a result of my not flying home for Aunt Sylvia's funeral," Jon said. "Believe me, I want to explain— "

"I prefer not to discuss it," she interrupted and turned to the window again.

Her anger with attorneys in general began during her dealings with the elderly attorney who'd mishandled her parents' wills, and was exacerbated by the fact that medical costs had almost decimated their small estate. And now Jon. It was unforgivable that he hadn't done his job as the estate attorney. He hadn't even cared enough to fly home from Europe for Aunt Sylvia's funeral.

She forced her thoughts from the matter, reminding herself that he was the only one she really knew in the older tour group. Her cabinmate-to-be, Beth Stillman, was thirty-nine and the only other "young one."

"Have you decided what to do with Aunt Sylvia's house?" Jon inquired.

"I'm not prepared to discuss it yet," she replied.

In truth, she'd love to refurbish the old Spanish hacienda *if* there was money left. Jon would undoubtedly try to dissuade her from rescuing the house from its last few years of neglect, but how she'd like to fill it with joy and a loving family of her own!

Still facing the window, she remarked, "I will say, I've wondered why Aunt Sylvia bought the ticket for this cruise. By then her doctor hadn't expected her to live long."

"It wasn't important to her if she missed the trip," Jon

replied, then hesitated. "Let's just say, she was excited about it in either case."

"I suppose so."

"Anne Marie, there's something I'd like to tell you..." His voice faltered.

"What's that?" Secretly, she hoped it concerned a good reason for his not being at her aunt's memorial service.

"The trouble is, I can't tell you yet," he said. "I know that sounds schoolboyish and ridiculous."

She drew a breath. "Well then, it seems to me it's your secret, isn't it?"

He raised his brows. "Seems it is."

"I think I know what it is."

"I hope so," he answered. He said nothing else.

She suspected her aunt had known Jon was going on this voyage and had connived to bring the two of them together. And then there were her aunt's strong Christian convictions—not that Anne Marie didn't believe in God, even if she rarely attended church.

Jon, she knew, was more devout. According to her aunt, he'd committed his life anew to Christ since his fiancée's death. She knew he'd had a lot to deal with. The accident had brought to light the fact that his fiancée had been running around with a married man. No wonder he still wasn't married.

Jon sighed with resignation and pulled out his briefcase. "May as well learn more about our destinations." He extracted a paperback about Greece from the briefcase and snapped the case shut again.

"I did a bit of research to refresh my memory before we left," Anne Marie responded. Studying about their tours had been interesting. It had also been a diversion from the legal complications.

He made no reply, and she gazed out the window again,

eager for the cruise to begin. Fortunately there would be a thousand passengers on their ship, the *Golden Isle,* when they boarded in Athens, and most of the passengers would be ordinary tourists like her, not religious pilgrims like those in the Santa Rosita group. And most important, one of them would be Alex Andropoulos.

Last month when she had read that the *Golden Isle* was part of the Andropoulos shipping fleet, she'd written Alex that she'd be aboard. "I'm eager to see you again," she'd written.

An understatement.

A remnant of a girlish dream.

For all she knew, he might even be married.

Now she looked away from the changing views of the earth from the airplane window and thought about his fax in her handbag. *Will be on ship,* he had replied. *Our "someday" has finally come.*

CHAPTER

Two

Athens! Anne Marie marveled as the plane descended in the gathering dusk. After reading voraciously about Greece in the past years because of Alex Andropoulos, she fully expected it to be one of the most interesting places on earth.

"It's as beautiful from the air as I remembered," Jon remarked from the seat beside her.

"And as I'd hoped," she replied, wishing he wouldn't lean quite so close to look out her window again.

Lights had begun to glow all over the city, and the highways were turning into luminescent streaks as the plane neared the airport. Finally the plane bumped down and roared along the runway while her mind repeated over and over, *Alex, I'm here! I'm here!*

She wondered if he'd be awaiting her at the airport. Would they recognize each other after so many years? And what would Jon and the others from Aunt Sylvia's church group think about her meeting Alex?

She'd have to deal with that soon, but it wasn't as if it had been a deception. They knew that she had inherited her ticket and was not a "pilgrim" in the same sense they were.

"Excited?" Jon asked as they unbuckled their seat belts.

"Yes! Thrilled is more like it!"

She stood up stiffly from sitting so many hours and smoothed her blue pantsuit. *Best not to mention Alex yet.* Instead, she said, "I've never been out of our country except on that one-day trip to Tijuana. Remember? You played tour director."

A smile lit his face. "That was a long, long time ago."

She nodded. "It was the first time I ever stayed with Aunt Sylvia, the year that Father died. You were kind to a mere teenager from Nebraska who still wore braces."

He laughed. "I'm usually kind to beautiful young ladies."

Far kinder than you've been lately—not even coming home from Europe to attend Aunt Sylvia's memorial service two months ago, she thought, trying to suppress her anger.

He seemed to study her face for a moment as he stood. "Mind telling me what's wrong? You've been cool since the trip began."

She gave him a slightly indifferent shrug. Silence hung between them as they started down the plane aisle with the other passengers. In addition to his avoiding the estate work, she felt he was somehow responsible for trapping her into taking this Holy Land trip. The expense of it—beyond the inherited cruise ticket—seemed especially unfair. *On the other hand, I get to see Alex.*

"You *are* angry." Jon moved in step beside her. "I suppose it has to do with my not flying home..." His voice trailed off.

"Let's not discuss it now. I'm tired of dealing with legal matters."

"I'm truly sorry, Anne Marie."

Perhaps she was being unfair to him, she decided as she made her way down the plane's aisle. If only she could be as forgiving as Aunt Sylvia had been. But it made her sad to think of her aunt. Grief was only part of the problem. Lately it seemed that her friends had scattered all over the country or married.

As they disembarked from the bus and made their way through the security check, she looked anxiously for Alex. No sign of him. No sign of him either as they passed through Greek customs.

Instead, there were beaming *Golden Isle* tour guides who directed them to waiting buses. "Welcome to Greece," an older guide called out. "Don't worry about your luggage," said a gracious young woman. "It will be taken directly to the ship."

Jon stayed at her side, but Anne Marie stepped up to the guide. "A man was to meet me."

"Perhaps he's on the ship," the man replied. "Airport security is tighter than usual lately."

"Yes, that's probably it." The security checks were making her feel more nervous than ever; likely Aunt Sylvia would say they reminded one of one's mortality. She tried to focus on meeting Alex.

"Meeting a friend?" Jon inquired. He stayed with her as they followed the older guide outside toward a distant row of buses.

"Yes, from years ago. Don't be such a lawyer. Curiosity, if you recall, killed the cat."

He chuckled. "All right. No third degree, I promise. I don't recall you ever being so prickly."

She smiled slightly. "I don't suppose you do." She walked in the dim light with their tour group toward the buses, trying not to be angry with him.

As she climbed into the bus, the Greek driver nodded graciously to her and smiled. *"Kalispera."*

"Kalispera." She was pleased to recall that it meant good evening. The driver beamed and Anne Marie was grateful to have memorized the few words given in the folders of information for the cruise. Alex would be pleased.

Jon was just behind her. She heard his pleasant Greek words to the driver.

She looked down the aisle at the passengers. Despite the long trip and the lack of sleep, the group from Aunt Sylvia's church was wide awake, their eyes bright with anticipation.

Spotting the last empty seat for two toward the rear of the bus, she wondered if she should head for it or take one of the single seats.

"Back there." Jon nodded to the empty double seat. "Just waiting for us."

Their fellow travelers overheard him, and there seemed nothing else to do but settle next to him. Her cabinmate-to-be, Beth Stillman, sat with Dr. Efrem Walcott in the seat behind it, and they smiled delightedly at the two of them. Anne Marie nodded, hoping they hadn't pegged her and Jon as a twosome just because they'd been sitting together.

"Ready for the great adventure?" Efrem Walcott asked, his booming voice enthusiastic. The group's leader for the trip, he was the pastor of the community church Aunt Sylvia had attended for years.

"I'm ready." Anne Marie slid her blue carry-on case under the seat. *Ready for anything,* she added to herself.

In truth, she felt a bit uneasy around Efrem, just as she did around all ministers, perhaps because she'd quit attending church when she went away to college. Still, Efrem Walcott was not only attractive with his thick dark hair and lively dark eyes, but apparently was also a great deal of fun. A recent widower and in his mid-fifties, he'd once been a well-known pro football quarterback. In his tan leather jacket and open-necked shirt, he in no way resembled her idea of a minister.

Beth Stillman was slim, of medium height, and as engaging as her bouncy brown curls. She'd worked in Efrem's office for the last six months. "Good friends," they called themselves, but from the glow on their faces, it appeared to be blossoming into far more. On the other hand, they seemed very careful of appearances, too. Efrem's wife had been bedridden for years, slowly withering away until she died nine months ago.

Several months after Efrem's loss, Aunt Sylvia had mentioned to Anne Marie that Beth was his new office secretary. "Efrem is withering away in sadness. I hope Beth will brighten his life. She's a joy."

Apparently Beth did make a difference, Anne Marie thought; *Efrem doesn't seem to be withering away now.*

"Here we go!" Beth called out as the lights dimmed and the bus took off. "Poor Efrem and Jon! Stuck with the two traveling innocents."

"What makes you think that?" Jon turned around and gave Beth a grin.

"Simple," Beth laughed. "Anne Marie and I were the only ones applying for our first passports!"

Efrem chuckled. "You two will manage if anyone can."

Anne Marie sat back, suspecting that Beth at thirty-nine was more like twenty at heart and that her enthusiasm would bridge their age difference. Despite years of working as a nurse and more recently caring for her sickly mother, Beth seemed joyously in love with life. Anne Marie couldn't help but envy her bright outlook.

"Thirty minutes to Piraeus," Jon said, settling back next to Anne Marie as the bus started off.

As they drove through the airport traffic, Anne Marie glanced out at lighted modern buildings, enjoying the exotic Greek letters on the many signs.

"It's all Greek to me," Beth laughed from behind them.

Efrem and Jon groaned good-naturedly.

Occasionally signs said *Pizzeria* or *Restaurant,* but most of the placards on even the modern buildings were written in the Greek alphabet.

"What's *ouzo?*" Anne Marie asked, noticing a billboard with the word in English and Greek. A handsome young man sat with a glass of a white drink in hand and a bottle on the table.

Efrem replied, "A liquor that apparently knocks one's socks off. The Greeks aren't known for drunkenness, though."

"I like them better already." Anne Marie glanced out the bus window as they passed by a street carnival and heard the calliope music. "Oh, look!" A colorfully lit ferris wheel circled high into the dark sky, and a bright tilt-a-wheel spun around and around. "That's the last thing I expected to see in Greece."

As they rode on, however, more exotic sights took over. On nearly every street corner, domed Greek Orthodox churches added to the foreign mystique.

"Over 90 percent of the people are Greek Orthodox," Efrem explained from behind them. "Most of the churches were bombed out in World War II, and nearly all of the port of Piraeus was lost, too, so this scenery is far from ancient."

When Alex had stayed with her family in Nebraska, he had told them about the war, even though it had been long before his birth. His parents had fled from Athens to the countryside, and several of his uncles had been killed in the resistance. The memory called to mind the great differences between her and Alex, and between their families.

"You're quiet," Jon observed. "Tired?"

"A little," she admitted, sitting back in the bus seat. She also found herself growing increasingly nervous as they rode toward Piraeus.

It seemed forever before they arrived in the port city, alight with modern apartment buildings, many lining the waterfront. Masts of yachts protruded from the lighted marinas everywhere, and in the distance, white cruise ships lay at dock, their lights turning them into floating palaces illuminated against the night. She reminded herself that no matter how dreamlike this might seem to her, this was part of Alex's usual world.

Despite their exhaustion, everyone in the bus strained forward to find their ship, the *Golden Isle,* among the line of beautiful cruise ships.

Jon spotted it first. "There she is!"

"It's...she's...beautiful, even more lovely than in the brochures," Anne Marie said, caught up in the burst of excitement with her fellow passengers. The *Golden Isle* was the most perfect place in the world to meet Alex again.

Outside on the dock, the damp sea air blurred the distant city lights, like a dark veil. *The Golden Isle,* however, was well lit. On the way to the gangway, Anne Marie rummaged in her handbag and dug out the glossy cruise ticket folder, her heart throbbing to the lively Greek music wafting down from an upper deck. Here she was with her two crushes from years ago suddenly in her life again. Jon walked beside her. And Alex waited somewhere to meet her. How unreal it seemed!

The enormous *Golden Isle* seemed equally unreal. Its bow rose gracefully in a sharp curve to the open decks above it. She wondered if Alex might be watching her from one of those decks. "I can't believe I'm here."

"That's how it always seems to me, too, when I travel." Jon said.

"I thought you'd be jaded after all of your traveling."

He grinned. "Not yet. Let's hope never! I can't bear jaded tourists. They ought to stay home. Come to think of it, I can't bear jaded people in general."

"Neither can I." For once, she returned his smile.

Moving forward in line, she craned her neck to see if Alex was at the top of the gangway, but there was no sign of him. Nor was he there as she stepped onto the ship. She impatiently endured yet another search of her handbag and carry-on case, then passed through another metal detector.

Finally she handed over her tickets to an elegantly uniformed ship's officer. Behind him, rows of white-uniformed crewmen stood at attention, moving forward smartly as the lead attendant stepped up to escort passengers to their cabins.

"Cabin thirty-three, Aegean Deck," the officer said and beamed at Anne Marie. He handed her key to the white-uniformed attendant who relieved her of her carry-on case.

"Follow me, please." His accent sounded like Alex's when he'd first arrived to live with them. The attendant's name tag read *Nikkos.*

She quickly glanced about the luxurious salon with its crystal chandeliers and plush gold carpeting. Still no Alex. Perhaps he was being circumspect, not wishing to draw attention to them by waiting here.

Anne Marie followed Nikkos through the salon, watching at every turn for Alex. Passengers crowded the corridors and elevators, some already studying their small deck plans.

"Aegean Deck, cabin number thirty-three." Nikkos stopped and unlocked the door for her.

As he opened it, Anne Marie quickly surveyed the cabin's beautiful white, gold, and green decor. The room held twin beds, a dresser, a mirrored makeup table, and a coffee table with two small upholstered chairs. One bed lay against a wall with a golden ceiling-to-floor mural of Greek soldiers on horseback; the other, against the porthole wall. It took a moment before she noticed the huge bouquet of dark red roses, at least two dozen of them, in a vase on the coffee table. Hurrying to them, she noted her name on the envelope. She tore open the envelope with trembling fingers.

Her heart leapt as she read the words on the white card. *Our "someday" has come at last. Alex.*

He hadn't forgotten! He hadn't!

"A telephone message." Nikkos nodded toward the glowing light on her phone.

She started for the phone, but Nikkos protested. "If you please, the life jackets..." He opened the closets, then showed her the tiny and sparkling clean bathroom. Anne Marie tried to be patient. Finally, his tour of the small cabin was complete. Knowing not to give tips yet, Anne Marie thanked him and reached for the phone.

Beth and her attendant stepped in the door. "My, look at the roses!" Beth's green eyes opened wide. "Did Jon send them to you?"

Anne Marie shook her head, grateful that the opportunity to tell about Alex had arisen so naturally. "They're from an old friend here in Athens."

At the phone, she punched in the ship's message number. Waiting, she watched Beth's attendant begin the same tour of the cabin.

A male voice spoke on the phone. "Operator."

Anne Marie felt caught off-guard by the Greek accent again. "The...message light is on for cabin thirty-three, Aegean Deck."

"Yes, a message for Miss Anne Marie Gardene."

"This is she." Anne Marie caught her breath and waited in anticipation.

"The message reads, 'I board at eleven. Meet me in the Ionian Lounge at midnight. Alex.'"

"Thank you." She hung up in disappointment. *Midnight.* Still, there'd be time to shower and eat dinner, and to compose herself. Though she wondered if that was possible at the rate her heart was thundering.

Beth closed the cabin door behind her attendant. "Everything all right?"

"Yes, just fine." She spoke quickly before Beth could probe further, "Would you prefer this bed under the porthole? It looks like the best for seeing out."

"No thanks, this one is lovely. Besides, I can sleep anywhere."

"The sleep of the innocent?" Anne Marie asked.

Beth lifted an eyebrow, then smiled. "I'm not so sure about that! There's an old saying that God gives sleep to the bad, too, so the good can rest undisturbed."

"I've never heard that."

Anne Marie sank down onto her bed and glanced at her watch. "It's almost seven o'clock Athens time!" *Five hours. Only five hours until she would see Alex.* Her heart still pounded.

"Thank goodness we're to wear casual attire for the buffet dinner tonight." Beth said. "I'm too tired to even change clothes." She hesitated. "By the way, Efrem and Jon have the cabin next door. They said they'd pick us up at seven-thirty."

"Oh?" Anne Marie turned to hide her dismay. She'd been right: people did think of her and Jon as a twosome. Her eyes wandered to the elegant bouquet of red roses. She'd have to explain about Alex tonight.

"Do you want to shower first?" Beth asked, sitting down on her bed with a sigh. "I'm being selfish, not noble. I'm hoping for a five-minute nap."

Anne Marie shook her head. "If you can merely lie down and sleep for five minutes, you're *entitled* to the second shower. I'm so excited that I may not be able to sleep the entire trip."

"Ah, youth!" Her roommate laughed and slipped off her pale green sweater and skirt. She pulled back the bedspread. "Would you wake me when you get out?"

"Sure thing." Anne Marie smiled. "Sleep well."

Anne Marie stepped into the small bathroom and realized how exhausted she was. Oddly, she felt pangs of the aching loneliness that so often assailed her. Why? Why would it rear its ugly head in the midst of this excitement and anticipation?

Especially now with Alex coming to meet her. Surely he wasn't engaged or married if he were joining her on the cruise.

In the shower, needles of hot water stung her, and she focused on how much her old friends in Nebraska would enjoy a trip like this. Many were already married, some with children; a few had blossoming careers. But remembering them only reminded her of how much they seemed to be drifting apart.

When she stepped out of the steaming bathroom, wrapped in a thick white towel, she was surprised to see that Beth was indeed asleep, her light brown hair spilling across the white pillowcase. She looked like a child, slight and defenseless, with a hint of a smile on her face, and so lovely that it was a mystery why she'd never married.

"Beth?"

Beth blinked awake and sat up with a smile. "Thanks." She yawned and stretched. "I feel better already."

Anne Marie marveled at her roommate's fast recovery. If only she could sleep like that! Sometimes she wondered if she couldn't because of her occasional nightmares. It was frightening to let go and drift off into the unknown. Perhaps it had something to do with so many deaths in her family in the last few years. No, she didn't want to think about it.

She noticed Beth watching her. "I still can't believe you can drift off to sleep like that."

Beth stretched again, luxuriously. "It's old age."

"You look like a teenager!" It was true; except for the smile lines around her mouth, it looked as if her roommate had never had a worry in the world.

"No thanks! I'm glad I'm this far on life's journey and more or less intact."

"Aunt Sylvia told me you'd been a nurse for years. I'm curious as to why you gave it up."

Beth heaved a sigh. "It was high time for a change, and I felt as if God wanted me to move on to more of a ministry. Besides, the hours for nurses are dreadful."

Anne Marie decided to ignore the matter of a *ministry.* "I hope you don't mind my asking, but were you Efrem's wife's nurse?"

Beth shook her head. "No, I don't mind your asking. You can rest your mind about it. I wasn't his wife's nurse."

Thank goodness! Anne Marie thought. "It was a rude question, but...well, I like you, and I didn't want to feel skeptical."

Beth gave a laugh. "I'm glad that you like me. And don't worry—you're not the first one who's asked. You probably won't be the last. People wonder. Everyone expects ministers to be far more moral than anyone else."

"Yes, I suppose so."

"It's important to us to keep the air clear."

"You mean important to Efrem and you?"

Beth nodded. "We don't want people saying, 'Just look at that minister—his wife's barely dead, and he's already dating his secretary.' Unfortunately, even the appearance of indiscretion can shake some people's faith."

"You're not seeing each other?"

Beth shook her head. "Mainly, we see each other in the office and on Sundays at church. His wife has only been gone for nine months, and some people still deem it proper to mourn for a year. Especially if the man happens to be a minister."

"I suppose that's true. On the other hand, I'd think a great deal of his mourning was done during the years his wife was dying. It's not as if she died suddenly."

"It sounds as if you know a good bit about mourning."

"More than I've cared to over the years," Anne Marie admitted. "I wish I hadn't brought up the subject."

Beth gave her a rueful smile. "I'm not. I'm glad the air is

cleared. Now I'll go take my shower. Efrem says they won't bring up the luggage until after dinner."

Anne Marie slipped back into her blue knit pantsuit, hoping that her luggage would arrive after dinner; she wanted to wear something smashing for Alex. Looking in the mirror, she smoothed back her hair. The chignon was holding up amazingly well, and the few blond wisps that curled around her face softened the severe effect. Considering how long they'd traveled, she didn't look too terrible, she decided, then turned to unpack her carry-on case.

Finished, she sorted through the ship's literature on the dresser: a one-page ship's newspaper, a deck plan, and pamphlets about the ship's shore excursions. It would take days to learn her way around, she thought, looking at the deck plan. The Ionian Lounge, where she was to meet Alex, was shown on the deck plan; it was apparently the ship's night club where the orchestra played dance music every evening. She smiled to herself, picturing the place where tonight she'd dance in Alex's arms.

Later, she and Beth were ready when Jon and Efrem arrived at the door, fresh-scrubbed and beaming.

"Look at those red roses!" Efrem's powerful voice carried out into the corridor. He turned to Anne Marie, his eyebrows lifting charmingly. "A secret admirer?"

"Not so secret now," she said, smiling at him, but added nothing more as she moved to the doorway.

"Ready?" Jon looked vaguely disconcerted as she came out into the corridor to join him.

She nodded. "Ready." It was the first time she'd ever seen Jon look unsure of himself. Was it because of the roses?

"I hope you don't mind my picking you up," he began, "but since we're in the next cabin and at the same table in the dining room..."

"Of course not," she assured him.

They followed Beth and Efrem through the long corridor toward the elevators. What woman could possibly object to being escorted by Jon Barnett? Not only was he terribly attractive, but a spirit of adventure often sparkled in his eyes.

"I'm eager to explore the ship," she said to break the quiet between them.

"We'll be lucky to find the dining room tonight." He chuckled, then pulled the ship's deck plan from an inside jacket pocket.

The elevator was nearly full of passengers on their way down to the dining rooms and, stepping in last, Jon could hardly avoid his nearness to Anne Marie.

"A tight squeeze," said a man behind them as the elevator doors closed. "Everyone hold your breath."

Anne Marie shot a sidelong glance at Jon and found him gazing down at her. The intensity in his blue eyes made her suddenly catch her breath. For a long moment it was impossible to turn away, and his arm moved protectively to her elbow to steady her as the elevator started down. Aware of his warmth and strength, it took her too long to realize that the elevator had stopped. She finally stepped off, her face flaming. What was the matter with her? She most definitely did not want to get emotionally entangled with Jon. Certainly not now.

His hand still at her elbow, she allowed him to guide her through the crowd. At the dining room entrance, she looked up to find him studying her tenderly.

"Good evening." The maitre d' escorted them into the festive room. "Tonight we are serving buffet-style to accommodate the various arrival times of our passengers. This way, please."

The long white buffet tables, laden with sumptuous culinary creations, boggled her mind. A tiered ice carving offered silver dishes of caviar, oysters, shrimp, and crab. Beyond, there were salads and relishes, then trays of freshly steamed vegetables, fishes, and meats. In the distance, another long white table held fruits, desserts, and cheeses.

"We certainly won't starve here," Jon chuckled.

"No!" Anne Marie laughed with him as she was given a plate from a black-suited waiter. She moved along the buffet table, accepting samples of crab, Greek salad with feta cheese, asparagus, airy potato puffs, bits of roast duckling, and a slice of prime rib.

Jon followed behind her, apparently as distracted as she was by the extravagant buffet.

At the end of the buffet line, waiters and busboys waited to carry the passengers' overflowing plates to their tables. "The 'footsteps of the apostle Paul' group," Jon told the waiter.

Anne Marie followed the waiter, wending her way through the beautifully set tables with white damask cloths and tall silver vases of pink and yellow roses. She thought again of the red roses in her cabin as the waiter seated her.

The two couples at her table greeted them, the men rising for her and Beth. "We're so pleased to have you join us," one of the men said with genuine enthusiasm.

Anne Marie was pleased to recognize that their tablemates were old friends of Aunt Sylvia who'd been at the pre-trip meetings in the church lounge. Rena and Reynold Williamson, newlyweds in their fifties, sat to the left of Jon. There were also the elderly Nathans, Kate and Nat, who'd taken a raft trip through the Grand Canyon last month and whose enthusiasm belied their ages.

Efrem Walcott settled into a chair on Anne Marie's right, with Beth on his opposite side. Everyone beamed their approval at Anne Marie and Jon. How could she possibly break the news about Alex? It sounded implausible that his family just happened to own the *Golden Isle* and several other cruise ships, not to mention tankers and freighters plying the oceans of the world.

Anne Marie felt even more uncomfortable sitting beside Efrem as he and Beth bowed their heads for a moment of prayer. She glanced at Jon, curious to see if he prayed too. Perhaps he had already, because now he waited for her to lift her fork.

She tried a bit of the chilled crab. "It's wonderful."

"Everything is," Rena Williamson laughed wryly. "I lost weight just so I could eat happily on this trip."

"You always look beautiful to me." Reynold, her husband, gave her an admiring look.

"Newlyweds!" Jon teased, and Anne Marie concentrated on slicing her prime rib to hide her smile. It seemed amazing that a couple in their fifties could look so adoringly at each other. But then, her parents often had, too.

"Athens tomorrow." Jon glanced at her as he lifted his fork.

Anne Marie nodded. "I can't really believe it yet. I've read so much about Athens." The time had come to say something about Alex; she couldn't delay forever. On the other hand, she didn't want to offend Aunt Sylvia's friends. They were all looking at her. "And I'm so excited to be almost there," she added quickly.

Everyone smiled, then returned to their eating and light conversation. From her side, Efrem asked quietly, "Is something troubling you, Anne Marie?"

Now, she told herself. *Now.* "Yes," She spoke quietly to all of them. "A friend of mine from Athens is meeting me, and I'm not sure I'll be touring with you tomorrow." She rushed on. "He was an exchange student and stayed with my family years ago. His name is Alex. Alex Andropoulos."

Reynold Williamson looked up from his plate. "Doesn't the Andropoulos family own this ship?"

She nodded. "Yes. Alex needed to hone his English before he went on to Harvard."

Efrem gave her a quick smile. "Well, that's wonderful for you. Don't worry about us. You'll have plenty of time to spend with us after Athens."

"I don't know. Alex booked himself on this cruise." She glanced up at Jon, but it was difficult to read his expression.

Efrem took a sip of ice-water, then placed the glass on the table. "If your friend Alex is interested, we'd be happy for him to accompany us on the land tours."

"Thank you, but I don't think so." Anne Marie gave Efrem a grateful look. "I'm sure he's seen most of the shore excursions often." No sense in telling them that in Nebraska, Alex had played soccer instead of attending church with her family on Sunday mornings.

She was thankful when the conversation moved on to the places they would visit: Athens, Corinth, Delphi, Crete, Istanbul, Ephesus, Patmos, Rhodes, Egypt, and Israel. As the supper continued, she was equally pleased to see what a congenial crowd they were, happily accepting her despite her impending defection.

When they stood up from dinner Jon asked, "Are you still interested in a tour of the ship?" His blue eyes seemed darker than usual. "We can make a start at learning our way around."

Anne Marie glanced at her watch. "I don't know..."

"Are you expecting your friend tonight?" He lifted a brow, but his expression was unreadable.

"Alex won't arrive until later tonight...and I would enjoy some fresh air."

Jon's voice was light. "We should be able to find that without too much trouble." He pulled the ship's deck plan from his blazer pocket. "Most cruise ships have a Promenade Deck."

As they pored over the deck plan together, it was obvious this was not Jon's first cruise. There was indeed a Promenade Deck.

After making their way up by elevator, they passed colorful boutiques, then found the outside door. They stepped from the ship's icy air-conditioning and bright lights into the warm October air and a velvety night.

Inhaling deeply, Anne Marie strolled to the gleaming railing and looked through the darkness to the dimly sparkling hillsides of Piraeus. "I still can't quite believe I'm in Greece. Does it seem like a dream to you, too?"

He didn't answer immediately and stood looking out at the lighted hillsides with her. "It doesn't seem quite real that we can be transported from one side of the earth to another in a day or two. From a contemporary cruise ship to ancient ruins."

She looked out at the night sky, then back to the lights of Piraeus. Alex could be in one of the cars that made up the golden stream of lights flowing from the highway.

"I'd like to tell you, after all, why I wasn't there to settle your aunt's estate."

She turned to see Jon gazing at her, his expression intense. "Another time, please, Jon. I'd really rather not discuss it."

"When you're ready, Anne Marie, I do want to explain..." His voice dropped off.

She shook her head briskly. Perhaps he could clear up the reasons for his absence, Anne Marie thought. Perhaps there was a logical explanation, but she didn't want to hear it now. Maybe never.

Leaning against the ship's railing, she turned again to the night sky and let everything else drift away—except, of course, Alex.

Jon still watched her as if trying to read her thoughts. "Would you like to walk?"

"Yes, thank you."

They strolled around the Promenade Deck, accompanied by other passengers.

"Beautiful, isn't it?" Jon asked, looking across the moonlit deck.

"Yes."

After several minutes, with Jon providing most of the talk, Anne Marie stopped abruptly, meeting his eyes. "I'm afraid I'm not terribly good company, Jon. I'm sorry, but I'd better get back to my cabin. Let's hope the luggage has arrived."

Her thoughts turned immediately to what she'd wear for dancing with Alex—the midnight blue silk dress Aunt Sylvia had sent her last year. "And I'd better hurry," Anne Marie added, suddenly nervous. In the dim light, she found her deck plan in her purse.

"May I accompany you?"

She shook her head. "I can find my way, but thank you for the breath of fresh air."

In her cabin, Anne Marie was glad to see their suitcases had been delivered. There was plenty of time to unpack and to get ready. She turned on the ship radio to romantic music and began to unpack. Shaking out her clothing, she decided the creases might hang out in the closet. The midnight blue silk, packed carefully with Alex in mind, was fine. She slid her unpacked suitcases under her bed, then still had a half hour to dress.

At a quarter of twelve, Anne Marie heard voices out in the corridor, then Beth let herself in. "Still here?"

"I'm to meet him in the Ionian Lounge at midnight."

"Sounds romantic." Beth smiled sleepily. "I'm dying to meet this Alex, but right now I'm ready for bed."

Anne Marie took a last glance at herself in the dressing table mirror. With her blond hair styled away from her face, her scoop-necked midnight blue dress, and high-heeled sandals, she looked far more sophisticated than usual, not at all like the naive young teenager Alex had known.

"He'll reel at the sight of you," Beth assured her.

"We'll see." Anne Marie arranged an errant strand of hair at her temple. "I'll try not to wake you when I return."

Slipping her key into her pearl-covered evening bag, she left the cabin, her dress brushing silkily against her skin as she hurried down the corridor.

In the elevator, the deck she sought was clearly marked on the control panel; she pushed the button, aware that the other passengers watched her curiously. Trying to contain her excitement, she finally stepped out on the Ionian Deck.

Romantic music swirled from the lounge as she made her way to the open doorway and peered into the dimly lit room. *What if Alex hadn't come after all? What if...*

Suddenly, there he was. Her heart pounded wildly.

Spotting her, Alex strode across the room toward her, his brilliant smile wide. He looked far more mature, yet not too terribly different. She'd have recognized him anywhere. His strongly chiseled face was, if anything, more handsome; the cleft in his chin was even deeper than she'd remembered; and the shoulders under his white shirt broader.

"Anne Marie..." His Greek accent added intimacy to his voice. "Anne Marie Gardene..." He reached for her hand, then kissed her fingertips.

"Alex..."

He gazed at her with bemused dark eyes. "You have most assuredly grown up."

"Yes..." She gave him a tremulous smile.

"Come." He took her arm. "Let me introduce you to my friends. It has been such a long time..."

She felt as if she were floating in a dream as she allowed him to guide her through the darkened room, accompanied by the orchestra's romantic music.

"Did you have a good flight? When did you arrive?"

As she answered, she thought how surprising it was that he would have friends with him now—tonight.

They stopped at a table with a view of the lighted hillsides of Piraeus on one side and the dance floor on the other. Alex pulled back Anne Marie's chair, and she seated herself.

"Anne Marie Gardene," Alex said, "may I present my good friends, Lila and Averill Thornton."

She felt an odd sense of insignificance when faced with the elegant couple. As Averill Thornton stood, she could see that he was an extremely tall, slender man with thin gray hair, possibly in his late sixties. Lila was a gorgeous redhead well into her thirties.

Acknowledging the introductions, Lila's smoky gray eyes narrowed into a calculating expression. "How do you do?" Her voice held a thick German accent.

Anne Marie had a strange feeling that the woman had totaled up the cost of Anne Marie's clothes and dismissed it as negligible, then guessed everything that Alex had not already told them about her, and dismissed it as negligible too. She suspected that her career as a kindergarten teacher would only elicit an indulgent smile.

Anne Marie nodded pleasantly toward the couple. "It's so nice to meet you." She quickly assessed Lila Thornton. The woman was not conventionally beautiful with her slightly hooked nose, but she was dramatically stylish in her deeply cut V-necked silk tunic and pants, looking as if she'd stepped from the pages of a fashion magazine. Her beautiful mane of auburn hair was gathered up in a turn-of-the-century topknot, giving her an incongruously old-fashioned appearance. Her makeup was as perfect as her hair and clothing.

"We have been hearing all about you and Nebraska." Lila said, then darted a defiant glance at Alex.

Anne Marie turned to Alex. "I've often wondered how you

remember your time with us."

"It was a wonderful experience." Alex lit a cigarette for Lila. "How could I not enjoy it? You were all so good to me, helping with my English, showing me about being an American..."

Averill smiled amiably. "Little effect it had on him."

Alex grinned. "A Greek is always a Greek, no matter where he lives. You can send him to Nebraska or to Harvard, but it is impossible to make much of a change in him."

Lila and Averill laughed, and Anne Marie joined in.

"A Greek is so Greek," Alex continued, "that when the Turks left this land after five hundred years of occupation, it was as if they had barely stayed one evening."

Lila shook her head in amusement, but he ignored her as he continued. "Even though the Greek language wasn't allowed to be taught in schools, every family taught it to their children. At home and quietly."

"Now, Alex," Lila put in, "it seems to me that Greeks are also blind. Or why is it more Middle Eastern in Greece than it is European? I suggest that the Turks left a good deal of their food, habits, and customs behind. Just look at the villages, how the women are treated—the men riding on donkeys, the women walking. Even in Athens the men sit over their coffee and *ouzo* while their women are working. The Greeks have turned part Turkish!"

"You're speaking heresy, Lila," her husband laughed. "If looks could kill..." He gestured at Alex, who scowled.

"Greeks are Greeks, and Turks are Turks, and never shall the twain really meet!" Alex put in, a touch of irony in his tone. "And Lila is always Lila." He lifted an eyebrow. "She likes to keep the pot bubbling, doesn't she?"

Lila darted a provocative look at Alex, and Anne Marie felt out of her depth.

The conversation finally became general, and she gathered

that Lila's main interests on this cruise were shopping and lying on the deck. Averill, an international banker, had taken the cruise because his doctor had advised it. Still, he intended to visit the archaeological sites. "I'm an archaeologist at heart," he explained to Anne Marie. "The trouble is that I discovered archaeology too late in life."

"You are a banker at heart," Alex grinned at his friend. "At least you seem so when loans come due."

"But not while I'm on holiday," Averill protested. "Now I consider myself an archaeologist."

"A banker," Lila said. "That is, of course, unless you don't ask how much I spend tomorrow."

Averill chuckled. "An archaeologist couldn't afford Lila. In fact, two former husbands couldn't afford Lila."

Lila gave a brittle laugh.

Anne Marie was grateful when they all sat back to listen to the music. Perhaps they meant to provoke each other as entertainment, but it made her uncomfortable.

Alex turned toward Anne Marie, his dark eyes assessing her. "What are you doing tomorrow? Will you be going to Athens with your friends?"

"I haven't made plans yet."

"Then tomorrow morning I'll show you Athens." His smile was warm. "And my mother insists that you have luncheon with our family."

"Thank you, I'd be delighted to, Alex." She tried not to sound too eager. Surely his family wouldn't invite her if he were married. "I still remember so much that you told me about your family—especially about Anna."

A hush fell over them, and she knew something was wrong.

Alex looked down at the table. "Anna is dead."

"I'm sorry! Oh, Alex, I'm sorry!"

"She had heart trouble for years. We always knew..." His

voice trailed off, then he looked at Anne Marie again. "I was sorry to hear about your parents, too. I should have written."

The familiar loneliness surged through her. "Thank you." The mere mention of them brought to mind her parents' uneasiness with Alex before he left, and she wondered what they would think of her being with him now. Wary. They'd likely be wary.

"You always reminded me of Anna," he said. "Not in appearance, since there she was quite your opposite with her dark hair and complexion. I think it was your air of innocence that I saw in her, too."

So that's how he saw me, Anne Marie thought.

He turned away. "Life goes on."

"Yes, life goes on."

How many others had spoken those very words in the past few years? *Life goes on. We have to go on.* And how often had she told herself that she was a survivor?

Alex understood.

No one spoke for a moment, then he filled the silence. "In the morning, I'll show you Athens as a Greek sees it, and at noon we shall dine with my family. In the afternoon I have last minute business affairs, but the company chauffeur could bring you back to the ship."

Happiness flooded through her. "It sounds perfect, but I don't want to impose— "

"Impose?" He laughed softly. "After my spending a whole school year with your family! What's more, they all want to meet you."

Lila and Averill had already told their plans: Lila would be shopping for raw silks to take to her London dressmaker, and Averill wanted to see the medieval wall recently unearthed near the Acropolis. They would not be along.

Alex's dark eyes met hers. "Now that we have tomorrow

arranged, would you care to dance?"

Catching her breath, Anne Marie nodded, then rose to her feet. As she preceded him to the dance floor, she wondered again if she were dreaming, but when she turned, Alex took her into his arms with a heartwarming smile.

"Oh, Alex," she murmured.

Her eyes closed at the wonder of his nearness, and he twirled her around the small dance floor until the Ionian Lounge spun around her. She felt deliriously happy.

"I knew," he said, his breath warm in her hair. "I always knew that someday I'd hold Anne Marie Gardene in my arms again."

CHAPTER

Three

The next morning Alex stood waiting for Anne Marie near the dining room entrance as planned.

His dark eyes softened with pleasure. "You look even more dazzling in the morning. As if that could be possible."

Anne Marie met his smile. She'd taken extra pains with her hair and makeup, and it was worth it now. "Thank you, Alex."

He held out his hand to escort her into the dining room.

If anything, he was the one who looked marvelous, she thought. His white suit contrasted with his green silk shirt and raven-black hair, setting off his good looks so much that he might have been a men's haute couture model.

As they stepped into the dining room, the dark, mustached maitre d' was immediately at their side, rattling off a Greek greeting to Alex, whom he addressed with great respect as "*Kirie* Andropoulos."

Alex answered in Greek, then explained to Anne Marie, "It's open seating for breakfast, but they have a private table for us." When he switched back and forth from Greek to English, she was pleased at how little accent he had in his English now. Apparently Harvard and the Gardene family of Nebraska had left their mark.

As the two of them moved through the vast roomful of elegantly appointed tables, she had the sensation of floating. Every table captain, waiter, and busboy seemed to be quietly aware of them; it was as if Alex were a prince and she a prospective princess for their realm. She noticed Jon at a nearby table with Beth and Efrem and sincerely hoped they didn't resent her defection, or her happiness.

"*Parakalo.* If you please." The maitre d' smiled, seating her with such a flourish that she was grateful to have chosen her one extravagant daytime dress, a sleeveless lavender linen with a matching cashmere sweater. It seemed suitable for the luncheon today with Alex's family, and it complemented her hair. It was a far cry from her teaching wardrobe, that tended to cute, colorful outfits.

Their waiter stepped forward with breakfast menus. His awe was so palpable that Anne Marie almost expected to be addressed as "your majesties." Leaving the menus with them, he backed away deferentially. She glanced over her menu at Alex with a barely contained smile.

"You find it entertaining, do you?"

She nodded. "Is it always like this?"

"Usually." There was a hint of amusement in his eyes.

"How do you live with it?"

"When you've had such treatment since birth, it seems normal. The unfortunate part is that you begin to expect special attention everywhere. When you don't get it, it's like a slap in the face."

"You weren't treated like this in Nebraska when you lived with us. You even mowed the lawn and took out the trash! We didn't know—at least I didn't—how importantly you were treated here."

He shrugged. "It was good for me to be treated like anyone else for a change. I could be a different person there, on the other side of the fence, as Americans say."

"Is that what I was to you? Someone from the other side of the fence?"

He hesitated. "Perhaps. Surely there's nothing insulting about that, is there? In fact, I find you refreshing. Far more genuine than most of the women I meet."

A white-jacketed busboy stepped forward to pour their coffee. Anne Marie took a sip, glancing up at Alex over the rim of her cup. "Thank you for the compliment, I think."

Was that how he had seen her years ago during those golden moments in the library? Refreshing? Genuine? What kind of women was he accustomed to now?

Turning to her menu, she put the thought aside. After all, Alex was a very eligible bachelor. All he'd ever done was hold her hand and whisper that haunting "someday."

Over breakfast he told her about his plans for his so-called inspection cruise on the *Golden Isle.* He'd stay with the cruise while visiting Greece and its islands, then rejoin them in Egypt and Israel. "It's an enormous responsibility, running a shipping line. My father's getting too old to handle it all. Slowly he's turning the reins over to me."

"Do you ever resent being drawn into the family business?" She took another sip of coffee. "Have you ever thought of being anything else—a doctor, a lawyer, an architect?"

"Since I was a boy, I realized this was the job for me. It's exactly what I wanted. It's a great challenge, and I've always enjoyed challenges. When I graduated from Harvard, my father gave me three ships to manage."

She gave him a knowing smile. "And I'm sure you did well with them."

He grinned. "I did. There's nothing like sound new ideas to improve a business."

"And you liked it?"

He gave a nod. "I was certain within a month that this was the life for me. I have no regrets."

Anne Marie dug her spoon thoughtfully into the wedge of ripe melon before her. "I'm surprised you haven't married."

He laughed. "It's not so unusual for an educated Greek to wait until he's thirty or even older to marry. As I said, I like challenges."

"You seemed happy in Nebraska," she said. "Was everything there a challenge to you?"

"Of course. It wasn't easy for an eighteen-year-old boy from another culture to fit into an American family and an American school. It was very different than what I'd expected. Very foreign to my ideas...to my whole upbringing. Didn't it appear so to you?"

"I...I suppose I was too busy with my own thoughts...too young to think about your situation."

He smiled broadly. "But you were not too young to think about love, Anne Marie."

She felt blood rush to her face and put down her spoon to hide her hand's sudden trembling.

Alex caught her hand and held it firmly on the table. "You're the right age to think about it now."

She recognized the passion in his eyes, the same look he'd had during their golden moments in the library. "It was a long time ago." Her voice was tremulous. "I thought perhaps you'd forgotten entirely."

"I remember." His expression was as warm as his husky

tone. "I remember now as if it were yesterday. At first you reminded me of Anna, but then I fell in love with that skinny bit of an American girl. It was strange. That last day in the library—it was as if you saw the stars reflected in me. I saw them in you, too. If it hadn't been for your father keeping us apart..." He didn't finish.

She felt a stab of sadness. *Yes, if it hadn't been for Father, what might have happened?*

Alex chuckled. "Then suddenly last month I received a letter from that skinny bit of a girl. She had a ticket on the *Golden Isle* and she hoped to see me!" He raised his eyebrows charmingly. "And my memories overcame me."

"Your memories?"

"My memories of a life less complicated, less sophisticated." He seemed lost in thought for a moment. "Still, I never imagined that my wholesome little Nebraska cornflower could have grown into anything so special. Then I saw you last night..."

She waited for him to continue, but he only smiled.

"Were you disappointed?"

"Not a bit, Anne Marie." His voice seemed to catch.

"Oh, Alex," she protested, even though it was precisely what she wanted to hear.

"No man could ever be disappointed in you." He lifted her hand to his lips.

The fleeting touch of his mouth brushing her fingers seemed to create a radiance all around them. *I always knew about you, Alex,* she thought. *I always knew you would be even more wonderful now.*

He raised a speculative eyebrow. "What is it about you that overcomes me so? Or is that how you affect all men?"

She smiled, shaking her head, torn between wanting desperately to believe him and agonizing over whether he was merely trying to flatter her.

"And you're a schoolteacher!"

"Yes, a kindergarten teacher. In fact, I've been thinking what I could buy for my teaching files—things to show the children."

"Ah, I'll have the New York office send you a giant poster of the ship and plenty of postcards of it sailing in the Greek islands."

"Wonderful!"

Later, as she and Alex walked down the gangway of the *Golden Isle* with the other disembarking passengers, she noticed the group from Santa Rosita had already boarded two of the nearby tour buses.

At the bottom of the gangway, Alex led her to a sleek red Ferrari, its motor running. "Here we are." An attendant hurried around to open the door for her. The buses with the Santa Rosita group pulled away, and she felt strangely relieved.

Alex shed his white linen jacket before he slid in beside her. She noticed the fine silk of his green shirt clinging to him here and there. It was already a warm day, and the coolness of the air-conditioned car felt delicious. Confined in its small space, she was intensely aware of him and caught his glance of assessment before he wheeled the car out of the parking lot.

"The tour of Athens begins." His grin was wry. "Although I may miss some of the usual tour guide talk."

"I doubt you'd miss anything." She was eager to start the day's adventure, unable to recall when she'd felt so happy. "What's on the agenda?"

"There's not time to show you much," he said as they pulled onto the main road through Piraeus. "I thought at least you could see the Acropolis and the Agora and maybe Syndagma Square. The tourists call it Constitution Square. You really should remain in Athens after the cruise is over." He turned to look at her, one hand on the steering wheel. "Perhaps we could change your airline ticket."

Anne Marie glanced at him in surprise. "Thank you. But... I don't know." It was tempting, but she hadn't even met his family. Moreover, she most definitely did not want Alex or his family to feel in any way responsible for her because he'd lived in her home in Nebraska.

As they drove, she gazed out at the hundreds of masts at the yacht marinas, then to the other side of the road where modern apartments with flower-bedecked balconies overlooked the nautical scene. Here and there elderly women shrouded in black hung out the wash—even on the elegant balconies—reminding her of Lila's comments about how Greek men treated their women. Her overwhelming impression of Greece by daylight, however, was of miles and miles of beautiful seacoast and marinas.

When they left the coast behind, Alex began a leisurely commentary on the sights. There was everything from fourth century B.C. temple ruins on unkempt vacant lots to the modern subway and dusty neighborhood squares with outdoor coffee shops where old, dark-suited men played backgammon. Whitewashed buildings climbed the nearby hillsides, and seafood restaurants edged the blue Aegean Sea. Everywhere children walked to school, both boys and girls in neat, white and navy-blue uniforms.

"Why do you smile?"

"I was trying to imagine you as a child. Did you wear a blue uniform, too?"

"We all did." He chuckled. "I was mischievous, maybe like that one there." He pointed to a boy who'd just tugged a girl's braid and was fleeing.

Anne Marie gave a laugh. "I'm not surprised! You were probably a handful for your teachers."

"I was." He grinned. "I'm afraid I was."

As they waited at a stop sign, she watched the nearby people. "It's so different here, yet the same, too."

"You mean the children?"

"No, more than that." She cast about for an example. "Like the signs on some of the buildings and billboards. I can't read the Greek letters except by connecting them with sorority and fraternity names at college. The signs and the advertising are the same, yet different."

"Yes, like all of the world," he observed, "the same in some ways but different."

As they approached Athens in the tumultuous morning traffic, she noticed more similarities to life at home. People bustled along the sidewalks, undoubtedly on their way to work. Taxis, trucks, and buses hurtled by, diesel fumes spewing into the air. Even the few dusty plants were like those at Aunt Sylvia's house in Santa Rosita: oleanders growing in hedges, hibiscus blooming in pots, red geraniums cascading from window boxes and balconies.

In the older neighborhoods, houses that were once handsome had fallen into disrepair. Seedy hotels, dreary shops, and cafés slowly gave way to the modern heart of the city, where tree-lined squares were resplendent with bright canopied tables and chairs, and taller marble buildings stood beside travel agencies and tourist shops.

"Oh!" Anne Marie cried out as a car careened maniacally toward them.

Alex blasted his horn, and the car veered at the last instant, honking into the cacophony of traffic.

She found Alex grinning at her white-knuckled hold on her

car seat. "How can you drive here?"

He laughed. "Only a Greek has the touch of insanity in his blood that lets him understand what another Greek driver might do next."

"That may be." But she didn't loosen her grip on the seat as they sped along through traffic. "That may well be!"

His answer reminded her of the previous night when he'd said, "A Greek is always a Greek." If that was true, what made them so different? Their history? Even here in the city, the past exhibited a prominence not found in Nebraska or California—ancient walls and other ruins between modern, high-rise office buildings.

Alex braked behind a huge silvery tour bus. "Ah, the Areopagus! I didn't even think to take you there."

"My tour group is going to see it. I think it's their first stop."

Alex contemplated the traffic with narrow-eyed concentration. "Then we most certainly must stop so you don't miss it."

"It's really not necessary," she protested, but Alex wheeled the car over to claim a parking space being vacated.

Quickly slipping out of her high heels, Anne Marie pulled on the tan sandals she'd carried along for sightseeing, then looked at the bustling scene around them. Parked tour buses lined the nearby streets, their blue, aqua, and lavender Greek lettering adding to the festive air of Athens. More buses snorted noisily into the lines, disgorging new tourists into the already teeming streets. Just beyond them stood a haven of parkland in the middle of the city.

"I still can't believe I'm actually here," she said as Alex opened the car door for her.

He laughed. "You are certainly here, and I'm glad of it."

Anne Marie laughed with him. "There's the Santa Rosita group starting up the hillside!" She waved at Beth, who must have told Efrem because he turned to wave at her, too.

"Your friends?" Alex asked.

She nodded. "My cabinmate and the minister."

"He's a minister? He looks more like a soccer player."

"Efrem was a professional football player. A well-known quarterback, in fact."

Alex raised his eyebrows slightly. "An odd road to becoming a minister."

"I thought so, too. I've been tempted to ask him about it, but it seems..."

"A rude question?"

She nodded. "Yes, a rude question."

As they made their way into the park, the morning sun was already warm and slanting through the olive, carob, and pine trees. Their fragrances overcame the stench of diesel fumes as she and Alex walked up the dusty knoll to the Areopagus. Near the top, a huge rocky outcropping stood, topped by a flat table rock that looked as if it had been provided by nature as an oversized stage.

"The Areopagus," Alex announced.

"What a sight!"

"You know of it?"

"Just from the tour brochures."

"Then you must know it's named in honor of Ares, the ancient god of war who was supposedly brought to trial here by Poseidon for killing one of his sons."

"I'm a bit fuzzy on Greek mythology."

"Who isn't?" He laughed, then continued. "In ancient days the supreme court sat here. They had a distinguished record of some thousand years in antiquity, so the name Areopagus was revived for today's supreme court."

"You're proud of your heritage."

He nodded. "Yes, I suppose I am."

"And rightfully, too."

"I might find humor in the old gods, but I feel an enormous pride in my ancestry."

"I'm glad to hear it," she said, though she didn't entirely mean it.

"Let's climb up to the top."

They joined the crowd moving toward the stone steps chiseled into the huge rock outcropping, and she thought of the thousands of men and women who'd climbed these same steps throughout the centuries. She extracted her small camera from her handbag, grateful she could capture these memories to bring out again years from now.

"The steps are uneven. Let me take your arm."

The grip of his arm under her elbow filled her with happiness and kindled an inner warmth. She recalled last night at her cabin door when he'd kissed her hand. She'd been surprised and not a little dismayed that he hadn't tried to take her into his arms.

As they reached the top of the stairs, she stepped out with him onto the rocky stage and found the view overwhelming. Across a narrow wooded valley, on a vast rock high above the city, stood the Parthenon. It was a magnificent sight with its tall white columns and ancient symmetry; it shimmered in the golden sunshine like a great crown.

"I didn't realize the Acropolis would be so separated from Athens."

"It was built as a citadel to defend the city."

"Then that makes sense," she said. "And now it's a citadel to the past, protecting the memories of ancient Athens."

"Exactly."

All around them, hills jutted from the earth, each with its

own name and interesting history, and Alex explained the panorama while Anne Marie took pictures.

"It *is* beautiful, isn't it? Sometimes I forget."

"Far more than just beautiful." Unfortunately the pall of smog hanging over the city saddened her, but she saw no point in mentioning it.

"Not like Nebraska?"

She smiled. "Not like Nebraska."

Anne Marie noticed the crowd around them on the hill was quieting, and she turned with them toward Efrem Walcott, whose resonant voice filled the air. "While the apostle Paul waited in Athens, he was upset by the idols he saw everywhere in the city, so he went to the synagogue and to the public square to discuss God with the Jews and the gentiles. He also debated with some of the Epicurean and Stoic philosophers. Their reaction, when he told them about Jesus and his resurrection, was 'He's dreaming!' or 'He's talking about foreign gods.'"

Anne Marie was certain Alex would not care to listen. "Shall we leave?"

He shook his head and murmured, "Let's hear what this football-player-turned-minister has to say."

Efrem continued, "They brought Paul to the forum here at the Areopagus, known then in Roman times as Mars Hill. 'Tell us more about this new teaching,' they said. 'You're telling us some strange things and we'd like to hear more.' As you might know, the Athenians, as well as the foreigners in Athens, reveled in discussing the latest ideas."

Alex chuckled. "That much hasn't changed."

Anne Marie smiled. As she turned, she glimpsed Jon close behind them, but he was so intent on Efrem's discourse that he seemed not to notice her.

His expression solemn, Efrem looked at the people standing

around him. "Paul stood before them here at the Mars Hill forum and said, 'Men of Athens, I see that you are quite religious. While I walked about, I saw your many altars. One of them especially interested me. Its inscription said, "To the Unknown God." Although you've been worshipping him, you evidently don't know who he is, and I'd like to tell you about him.

"It is he who made the world and everything in it. Since he is Lord of heaven and earth, he doesn't live in temples made by man. Our human hands can't minister to his needs for it is he who gives life and breath and everything else to all of us. From one man, Adam, he created all of the people of the world and made them live across the earth. He decided beforehand which nations should rise and fall, and when."

Efrem's voice was so compelling that even strangers coming to the top of the hill stopped to listen. Anne Marie's gaze wandered back to the Acropolis.

"'God's reason for all of this,'" Efrem went on, still quoting Paul, "'is that man should look for him, that we should find him, although he is never far from us. Someone has said, "In him we live and move and are!" And as several of your poets have said, "We are the children of God."' Since we are his children, we shouldn't think of God as an image made of gold or silver or sculpted of stone. He has overlooked our past ignorance of these things, but now he wants us to put away such idols and to turn from our evil ways.'"

Efrem paused as if to place emphasis here. "'God has set a day for judging the world justly by the man he has appointed; he has pointed that man out by bringing him back to life again.'"

Efrem smiled at his contemporary crowd. "When the Athenians heard about the resurrection of a dead person, you can imagine their laughter. Yet some said, 'Let's hear more about this later.' That ended Paul's discussion, but several of them including Dionysius—a member of the city council—and a woman named Damaris joined him, becoming believers."

When Efrem finished, a long reverent silence followed. After a while, the murmur of voices intruded on the thoughtful quiet, and people turned to descend the hill in the warm sunshine.

"He's good," Alex said. "Very convincing if you believe that sort of thinking."

Anne Marie fell silent, strangely moved. She believed, she truly believed, much of what she'd learned in Sunday school as a girl, but somehow her religion always seemed to drift away because of life's complications.

Alex took Anne Marie's arm as they turned to leave. "My mother had all of us in church as children. But that was enough. She has sufficient faith for the entire family."

Anne Marie recalled hearing something about God having no grandchildren, that the faith of family members did not lift others, that everyone had to find his own way to God.

As she took a last look at the Parthenon, she noticed Jon was watching her and Alex. She nodded pleasantly, deciding against introducing them in this crowd, then accepted Alex's hand to help her down the ancient steps.

Descending from the hill, it came as a shock to hear the noise of twentieth-century traffic.

"I'm grateful we stopped," she said as they made their way through the throngs of tourists on the sidewalks to Alex's car. "I'd have always thought I'd missed something."

"We visited here as school children for a Greek history lesson, of course. But I've often wondered about the many Christian tourists who come here. Now that I've heard the way your minister put it, it's more understandable."

Judging by Alex's slightly disparaging tone, Efrem Walcott's words had made little impact.

The red Ferarri was stifling hot inside, and they opened the windows as they drove off, letting the breeze cool them until the air-conditioning took over.

As Anne Marie looked out across the city with its tall, narrow cypress trees dotting the hillsides, it still seemed impossible she was here with Alex. She noticed that women on street corners and in passing cars took an interest in his dark good looks and that he seemed to enjoy the attention.

Driving through the crowded city, they neared the base of the Acropolis on narrow cobblestone streets where houses and shops were jammed tightly together. "This is the *plaka*, the oldest part of the city," he explained. "Tonight, if you like, we'll come here with Lila and Averill, then go to a *taverna* in the suburbs for dinner and Greek dancing."

"I'd love to," she answered, though she'd have much preferred to spend the evening alone with him.

After Alex parked, he guided her through the busloads of disembarking tourists, then the raucous vendors who sold postcards, sponges, and local handicrafts. "Parthenon! Parthenon!" they shouted, waving soapy-white models of the ancient building. "Buy the Parthenon!"

"No, I shall not buy the Parthenon!" she laughed and snapped the vendors' pictures. She and Alex moved on to the Acropolis admissions gate, then climbed the steep incline toward the Propylaea, the magnificent vestibule that rose before them. Alex helped her up the monumental blocks of marble serving as steps. Above them stood the towering pedestal known as the monument to Agrippa.

"It's even more impressive than it seemed from a distance." She snapped more pictures, feeling as if they stood in the midst of history.

Beyond was a glorious view of the Parthenon, its honey-colored columns of marble rising high over the ancient city. And there was the great central avenue of marble where processions of ancient Greeks once walked; where animals were led to be sacrificed to the gods. The reflection of light thrown back by the rocks and marble was as blinding as the panorama was dazzling to behold.

She caught Alex smiling at her, and she laughed. "You might think I'm terribly naive, but at the moment, I don't even care."

"You're a nice change from the jet setters I usually take about. So many of them are like Lila and couldn't care less. Fortunately, she's the first to admit it. Honesty is one of her virtues."

So, he'd shown Lila around, too.

Anne Marie bit her lip as she looked out at the city below, reminding herself that Alex had probably shown many women around. It was none of her business.

When they left the nearby museum, she saw Jon in the crowd by the Propylaea. She quickly turned away. It seemed as if he were following her, but that was ridiculous. The Acropolis had been the next stop on the agenda for his group, too. Later, she was relieved that he was nowhere in sight at the Theater of Dionysos or the gleaming white Agora restored to show life in Greece's golden age.

"Last year Lila and Averill came for the summer theater here. They still perform the ancient plays, as much for the tourists as for us Greeks. Averill enjoyed it all enormously. Lila went to sleep."

"One hears that opposites attract," Anne Marie said.

"Indeed. Particularly in that case. Lila's mother pretended to be a contessa. At least Lila has no such pretensions."

Not knowing how to respond, Anne Marie concentrated on

taking pictures and trying to put Lila out of mind. Surely Alex wasn't involved with a married woman.

It was nearly noon when they drove around Constitution Square. "Hundreds of tourists and Athenians used to sit at colorful outdoor cafés in the center of the square. Now we have a metro." He pointed out the deluxe Grand Bretagne Hotel, the nearby King George, and the large handsome building that had once been the royal palace.

He gave a laugh. "We once had to dodge waiters who rushed across the street with trays full of glasses. And now it seems like other cities."

"Not to me." She looked around her, trying to take in everything.

"I'm glad to hear it." He smiled at her again. "It's good for me to see the city with new eyes."

"Where to now?"

"We're headed for my family's city house, which is, alas, in the suburbs."

Her thoughts wandered to the imminent luncheon with his family. Surely they'd invited her only because he'd lived with them in Nebraska; she must not read anything more than that into it, much as she would like to.

She glanced at Alex, and he reached for her hand, giving it a firm squeeze. "My family will admire you. My mother is especially impressed that you're on a pilgrimage."

"A pilgrimage? Oh, no." She laughed quietly. "I inherited the ticket."

"I see." His expression seemed to brighten.

She remembered what he'd said about his mother having enough faith for the entire family. Perhaps she'd be one of those pious, little old Greek women shrouded in black.

He laughed. "You don't have to tell my mother about inheriting it. She's more interested in it being your pilgrimage."

Later, as they drove through the fashionable suburb of Kifissia, she changed her opinion as to what his mother might be like. The neighborhood was most elegant; instead of apartments and townhouses, each residence had an extensive garden, and trees shaded the grounds. She slipped on her high heels as Alex drove toward an entry lined with feathery pine trees. As they approached, Alex pressed a remote control button and tall iron gates opened electronically to admit his car.

Anne Marie's nervousness grew. She'd expected a lovely home, but nothing had prepared her for this white marble mansion with its classical Greek architecture and stately columns.

As she followed Alex from his car, the scent of jasmine and lavender wafted through the soft warm air. Heavy double doors at the entry opened, and a white-coated manservant waited to escort them indoors.

After greeting him, Alex escorted Anne Marie through the marble-floored entry to the salon. It was so enormous that it might have been used for great state receptions.

Her next impression was of whiteness and light from the walls. Silken draperies had been pulled aside to let sunlight stream through the french doors. The white marble floors were covered here and there by huge oriental rugs with antique furniture grouped about them. A profusion of flowers filled the room with color: pink and white roses, deep burgundy dahlias, varicolored gladiolus.

A slender gray-haired woman wearing a fashionable white silk dress rose from an overstuffed sofa. Smiling graciously, she hurried to Anne Marie.

"My mother," Alex said with a nod. Anne Marie had already known; there was something of Alex about her features, but with a softness of expression, a kindness in her brown eyes.

"It's such a pleasure to meet you, Anne Marie." Mrs. Andropoulos leaned forward to kiss her, first on one cheek, then on the other. "You were all so very good to our Alex in the States that I almost feel you are my daughter."

Anne Marie still felt overwhelmed by Mrs. Andropoulos's affectionate greeting as she was introduced to Alex's father, then his three older sisters and their husbands. Though friendly, they merely shook hands and greeted her in English.

"You have British accents," Anne Marie said, surprised.

Alex laughed. "Most of us had imported British tutors instead of going to the States. Anna and I had American tutors, and then of course I came to Nebraska."

"Earlier on, it was far more convenient for us to have British tutors," his father explained. "Tell me, please, are you enjoying the *Golden Isle*?"

"Yes, it's wonderful." Anne Marie smiled at the older man. "I have a very nice cabin." As she spoke, she recalled what Alex had said. His father was indeed elderly and had dark circles under his eyes.

Mrs. Andropoulos said, "Ah, here comes Marina!"

Anne Marie turned to see a manservant escort a slender young woman with lustrous dark hair into the room. She watched Marina's onyx eyes dart to Alex, who looked startled to see her.

Who is this? Anne Marie wondered, as Alex kissed the girl's hand. Marina was probably no more than sixteen, far too young to be friends with Alex's sisters. A cousin perhaps? In any event, she was lovely in a dark Grecian way.

Alex brought her to Anne Marie for their introduction. "Marina Zafis," he said, "this is Anne Marie Gardene. I stayed at her parents' house when I lived in Nebraska."

Marina extended her hand. "How do you do?" She seemed wary.

"How do you do?" Anne Marie smiled pleasantly, but the girl's dark eyes darted away.

Fortunately, an aproned maid waited to offer them drinks from a large silver tray, and Anne Marie accepted a glass of lemonade. Another maid arrived with a tray of hors d'oeuvres which Alex's mother explained. "These are *sanganaki,* fried cheese cubes, and here are *keftedakia,* lamb meatballs, and *pyropitakia,* our favorite cheese puffs."

As Anne Marie tried the delectable appetizers, she noted that Marina stayed close to Alex. By the time he escorted both of them into the palatial dining room, Anne Marie wondered if there was something special between them, but the girl was far too young for Alex.

During the soup course, Anne Marie learned from the brother-in-law to her left that Marina's father also owned a shipping line. Anne Marie felt another moment's uneasiness when she noticed that Alex was dividing his attention carefully between Marina and her, though he talked to the girl as if she were a younger sister.

After the salad course, Alex's mother said to Anne Marie, "We hope you will like *arni me fasolakia.* It is lamb with green beans and new potatoes. We thought it best not to start you with unusual foreign dishes at the beginning of your trip. There is quite enough of that when one travels."

"I'm sure I'll like it." Anne Marie watched the maid fill her plate with the delicious smelling casserole.

Alex launched into a discussion of his becoming accustomed to foreign foods in Nebraska. "The food was quite international. One night Italian spaghetti, the next it might be German or French cooking, then Chinese. I remember your mother made dolmades and moussaka to make me feel at home."

"That was most gracious. I wish we could somehow reciprocate for you," Mrs. Andropoulos said.

"Oh, but this is lovely," Anne Marie protested.

"It's nothing, nothing compared to what your family did for Alex," she continued. Her husband looked at Anne Marie approvingly, too.

She thought they might suggest her staying on with them for a week after the cruise, as Alex had mentioned, but nothing was said about it. The conversation moved on to the *Golden Isle*'s ports of call, and she smiled her way through the main course and the baklava dessert.

When they finally rose from the table, her eyes met Marina's for a disturbing moment. She couldn't fathom the expression in the girl's dark eyes. It had been such a cordial meeting with Alex's family, but there was something vaguely disquieting about Marina Zafis's presence.

CHAPTER

Four

The Andropoulos's long limousine stopped in the dockside parking lot near the *Golden Isle* at precisely two o'clock, and Anne Marie was out of her door before the liveried chauffeur could get out to assist her.

"*Efcharisto!* Thank you!" Anne Marie called back to him, grateful that the ship's daily paper had included a few Greek words to learn this morning.

She rushed for the tour buses parked near the ship. Several were already pulling away, black smoke billowing behind them, and she would have to stay on the ship if she missed the bus. Spotting two silver buses with *Footsteps of Paul* signs in the front windows, she ran for the closest one. As she climbed on board, the driver nodded at her while he started the motor.

Beth smiled at her from the front seat where she sat with Efrem. "You made it!"

"In fine style, I might add," Efrem joined in the welcome. "But you made it!"

"Barely!" Anne Marie's reply was breathless from her hurry.

She smiled at the Greek woman behind the driver, apparently their guide for the trip to Corinth. The bus was hot, even with the windows opened wide to catch the afternoon breeze from the sea.

"Anne Marie..." Jon stood in the middle of the bus. "Back here. I've saved a seat for you."

She started down the aisle toward him, aware of the curious glances directed at her. Everyone had noted her conspicuous arrival, and she felt like a traitor for touring in an air-conditioned limousine when they'd been suffering in the sweltering bus all morning. And here was Jon, saving her a seat again. She sighed as she made her way toward him.

"I'm glad to see you made it." He smiled pleasantly and waited in the aisle to let her pass to the window seat. He wore dark blue bermudas and a light blue polo shirt that heightened the color of his eyes and displayed the appealing breadth of his shoulders. Even when dressed casually, he gave the appearance of a gentleman.

"I'm afraid the air-conditioning on this bus has a mind of its own," he said.

She nodded. "It feels like it." She settled into her seat. "Did you have a good tour of Athens?"

"A fast one. If I hadn't spent time here on business several years ago, I'd have been completely overwhelmed."

She made no reply. If he thought she'd be impressed by his international law work, he was in for a surprise.

"How was your morning?"

She smiled. "Overwhelming."

His voice sounded somewhat strained. "I'm sure that your friend Alex is an excellent guide."

"He does know his way around Athens, but then he's lived here most of his life."

"You met his family?"

She nodded and smiled again. "Yes." Beth had probably mentioned the luncheon.

Jon appeared to be hoping for further details, but Anne Marie decided not to share anything further about Alex or the Andropoulos family, except perhaps later to Beth. In truth, her visit to Alex's family had been too exciting not to tell someone.

"It's just over fifty miles to Corinth," Jon remarked as the bus pulled out of the parking area.

"A chance for us to see the Greek countryside."

"Yes. Haven't you seen any of it?"

"Only a few suburbs."

Grateful for the breeze through the bus windows, she looked out into the brilliant afternoon light over the blue sea. Jon surely was curious about her morning.

In the front of the bus, the Greek guide began to give details about the passing city on her microphone. "Most Greeks take four-hour siestas during the heat of the day and work late into the evenings. As you see, many of the shops are closed."

Was that Alex's important business this afternoon? Anne Marie wondered. *A nap? Well, it is none of my business. No more than my outing with Alex is any of this group's business.*

In the suburbs, the guide discussed the history of Greece. When her commentary wound down, Anne Marie and Jon chatted about the passing scenery, the country's more recent history, ancient Greece, and the current language, until they somehow found themselves discussing the origins of words.

"Do you know what your name means?" Jon asked.

Anne Marie shook her head. "No, though it seems that I did at one time."

"Anne comes from the Hebrew name, Hannah," he said. "It means 'full of grace, mercy, and prayer.'"

"How did you know?"

He shrugged. "One of those bits of information."

She started to remember. "As I recall, Hannah of the Bible was the barren woman who, after praying in the temple, conceived the great prophet Samuel."

"Ah, so you do know something of the Bible," he said.

"A little from Sunday school. And I remember now that Marie comes from the Hebrew name Mary, or Mara, which means 'bitter.'"

"Your aunt must have told you."

Surprised, she asked, "Did Aunt Sylvia tell you what my name means?"

"She did. In fact, she often discussed you with me. You were like a daughter to her, you know, since she never had children."

Anne Marie swallowed at the thought of her aunt. "She was like my second mother. How did she happen to tell you the meaning of my name?"

"I suppose it was because she was concerned about how you'd turn out after losing both parents. How you'd react. You do have a double-edged name. Would you be an Anne—full of grace, mercy, and prayer? Or would you turn into a Marie—full of bitterness?"

It was annoying to hear that she'd been discussed so freely. She brushed away a bit of lint from the skirt of her lavender dress. "What do you think?"

"I'm not sure. Your aunt thought you were still bouncing along on life's middle road. Your outcome concerned her more than you can imagine."

Even more resentment rose to her throat. "And what does Jonathan mean?"

"It means 'gift of the Lord' in Hebrew."

A tinge of asperity crept into her tone. "Is that how you see yourself?"

His color deepened, and she felt remorseful. Jon had never acted superior—older perhaps, but never really superior. She took a deep breath, thinking she should apologize. Instead she said nothing.

"I don't feel that I'm 'a gift of the Lord' in the way you seem to be implying." He gazed past her out the window. "In fact, I fought that very meaning for years. I didn't want to be a 'gift of the Lord'—let alone the namesake of the best friend of King David."

"And how do you think you've turned out?"

He looked at her seriously. "Once you have a personal relationship with the Lord, that's the beginning of a new life and a new path. Unworthy as I am, I'm set on that path for eternity now."

She sat back uneasily. Did that mean he considered himself one of those born-again people? She certainly hoped not.

Aunt Sylvia had said, "I didn't dream Jon would fall in love with a young woman like Sondra, though she was beautiful—a runner-up in a Miss America pageant. Of course, opposites do attract. I suppose he was rebelling against the status quo just then, against his family background. The situation surrounding Sondra's accident was hushed up as much as possible. It was terribly sad for Jon, but it did bring him back to the Lord."

As Anne Marie recalled, she had made no response. She'd been in college then and living more decently than most students. She wasn't a liar or a thief. Nor was she promiscuous. She hadn't needed religion as a crutch, although Aunt Sylvia had called Christianity more of a pole vault into adventure.

Anne Marie ventured, "Just before she died, Aunt Sylvia mentioned that you recently came back to the Lord."

"Yes," Jon admitted, "I did."

"I see."

He was smiling at her, his blue eyes twinkling with interest, but he apparently was not going to divulge more unless he was questioned. Well, she wouldn't pursue the matter. As far as she was concerned, one's religion or lack thereof was one's personal business, and to be entirely honest, she had no right to pry into Jon's faith, either.

Glancing out the window, she wondered about others who were making this pilgrimage in the footsteps of the apostle Paul. Their measure of faith seemed to differ, not just with these so-called pilgrims, but among people in general. There were those who wanted to hear nothing about God and others who seemingly wanted to hear nothing else. Then there was the great crowd between those extremes. She supposed she stood somewhere in the middle. Not bitter like a Marie. Not full of grace, mercy, and prayer like an Anne, either. No doubt she was—as Aunt Sylvia had said—traveling along on life's middle road. Most likely, it was the safest and the sanest place to be.

For a long time they sat looking out at the passing countryside. Eucalyptus trees edged the roads, and here and there, the wind rippled fields of wheat like waves in great golden rivers. Slowly the landscape changed to rows of olive trees framing a vista to the bright blue sea. The scene was so breathtaking that she wished she could stop to savor the beauty, to fix it in her memory forever.

After a while Jon drew her attention to the view on the other side of the bus. "Gypsies!"

She looked out the windows across the aisle at the gypsies who lived by a city dump where, according to the guide, they mainly picked through the garbage for food and clothing.

"Why does God make them live from the dump?"

Jon grinned a little. "He's given us all free will to make our own choices. That means everyone from the rulers of countries to those gypsies. Everyone's choices impact others' situations."

Anne Marie turned away, unwilling to go more deeply into the matter. She could, to some extent, see the truth of it in her own life. For example, her choices as a teacher impacted every child in her class. If she started the day bright and cheery, her children often had a delightful day. If she was glum, that attitude rubbed off, too. If she was enthusiastic about a subject, the children often became enthused about it, too.

Farther along, there were black goats in pens, and the guide said, "These goats are the source of Greece's famous feta cheese. You have all had our feta cheese on the cruise ship?"

Her question brought an enthusiastic yes from the passengers.

The bus slowed, then the driver wheeled it to the roadside behind five other tour buses. The guide explained over her microphone, "We are on the outskirts of both the modern and the ancient cities of Corinth. Corinth, of course, is best known through the book of Corinthians in the Bible. You have twenty minutes for walking over to the bridge to look at our famous canal. There is a store here for buying drinks and souvenirs."

It appeared she was not going to give them a biblical lecture, Anne Marie thought gratefully. "Don't wait for me," she said to Jon as everyone started off the bus. "I'm changing shoes."

"I'll get us something to drink."

He was already making his way down the aisle with the others, and it seemed pointless to protest. Besides, she was thirsty. She pulled off her high heels and put them into a plastic bag. Her tan sandals, though far from elegant, were just the thing to explore the countryside.

When she climbed off the bus, Jon awaited her with two Styrofoam cups of lemonade. Others were watching and, despite everything, she found herself smiling. "Thank you, Jon. It's thoughtful of you."

"My pleasure."

She nodded. He'd gone out of his way to mend any bad feelings between them, and she decided that if nothing else, she could at least be friendly during the trip. It would make things far more pleasant.

The lemonade quenched her thirst as they stood in the

shade, admiring the hilly scenery. When they'd finished and disposed of the Styrofoam cups, they fell naturally into step in the hot sunshine, following busloads of tourists along the road to the bridge.

"I vaguely recall learning about Corinth, but I can't remember ever reading about the canal itself, except in our travel brochure." She remembered that Alex had mentioned it too.

"The canal wasn't here during ancient times," Jon said, "though it was under discussion even then. From what I remember, slaves transferred entire ships' cargoes to oxcarts and moved them across the land from ship to ship. Sometimes the ships themselves were hauled from sea to sea over a track with rollers. I imagine a canal was an appealing idea."

"Come to think of it, I do recall one thing. Julius Caesar had Mark Antony and Cleopatra pursued across here."

"And how do you know that?" He grinned at her.

She laughed. "It's the kind of thing a girl is apt to recall from history classes."

Their pleased guide spoke from behind them. "I've been...how do you say...eavesdropping. You two are very knowledgeable. Actually Nero started the canal. It's said that he cut the first sod with a spade of gold."

Anne Marie's eyes widened appreciatively.

Jon nodded. "As I recall, a rebellion in Rome stopped the building program."

"Exactly," the guide said. "The canal building wasn't taken up again until 1882. How do you two happen to know so much about it?"

"We've studied some history." Jon winked conspiratorially at Anne Marie.

It was true, and she'd always enjoyed history. She recalled the paperback Jon had been reading about Greece on the plane. He'd always been interested in everything, which was likely why Aunt Sylvia had willed him her extensive collection of books on history, philosophy, and religion.

As they stepped onto the long bridge, the narrow canal loomed before them, its depth making Anne Marie slightly dizzy. Tourists from the other buses already lined the bridge railings, marveling at the nearly perpendicular cut through the solid brown rock. A white cruise ship moved slowly behind a tug in the narrow blue waterway, and cameras clicked all around.

"During World War II, the sides were blown up by the retreating Germans," a young guide was explaining to his group of tourists. "It took many years for repairs."

"I'd think so!" Anne Marie remarked to Jon.

It occurred to her that this was why so many people traveled to ancient sites: to touch the past, to reach through the centuries for history to come alive. "Isn't this a wonderful sight?"

His blue eyes held hers. He nodded, though his tender gaze was on her. "Yes, a wonderful sight."

For an instant it was as if she were a girl again, seeing him for the first time on Aunt Sylvia's patio. She tried to shake off the memory and quickly stepped toward the ledge. "I'm going to take some pictures."

Their guide spoke on and on about the canal, but the words failed to register in Anne Marie's brain. Disconcerted, she tried to concentrate on the vistas in her viewfinder as she snapped pictures. But Jon's image—the tender expression on his face as he scrutinized her—wouldn't flee her mind. Her turmoil over him was distracting, and she was almost grateful when it was time to return to the bus.

Later, when the bus let them off at the ruins of ancient Corinth, she was careful to stay in the midst of the group. For years she'd longed for attention from Jon, but now it was too late. Simply too late. It was a peculiar way to make amends, but then maybe he was simply offering a few kind words and looks in lieu of an apology.

Not too far from the ancient ruins were small rock houses painted white. Sunflowers and orange trees stood in the dusty yards. Beyond the houses and across the fields was the blue Bay of Corinth.

Anne Marie's eyes turned to the Acropolis of Corinth, high on a distant hill. This was where the infamous temple priestesses-prostitutes had lived and practiced their religion—an unnerving sight for a woman and a dreadful idea of religion. Nonetheless, she focused her camera on the view.

The guide said, "The Acropolis is two thousand feet above ancient Corinth. You see the ruins of the crusaders' fortress there on the top like a crown. If you climb up to the top, you have the widest and most glorious view of all Greece."

"Someday I'd like to come back and climb to it." Jon said. "I understand you do some climbing."

"Yes. It'd be interesting." Perhaps Alex would bring her someday.

"Next year?" Jon asked. "We could come next year."

"We?" She laughed. "I don't think so."

Slowly, as they wandered through the ancient ruins, the air of camaraderie grew between them again. She was determined to keep it exactly that—camaraderie.

The guide pointed out the remnants of Roman baths, shops, fountains, and houses, some with sections of mosaic floor still intact; all had been built on top of the original Greek ruins, even using the same stones. As they passed the ancient Fountain of Peirene, everyone pressed their ears to the stone to hear the sound of water still bubbling there.

Anne Marie looked up at Jon. "You really can hear it!" Again, she found him watching her far too intently. She quickly turned away from his blue eyes.

Later, in the small museum, she could scarcely keep her attention on the archaeological artifacts with Jon observing her so closely.

Stepping out of the museum, Efrem Walcott caught the guide's attention. "Let's go to the area where Erastus's name is cut into the road. Do you know it?"

"Of course!" She nodded happily.

The guide led them through the ruins and straggly bushes to the remains of an ancient road where the Greek letters of the man's name were clearly cut into the pavement.

Efrem explained, "The book of Romans mentions Erastus, the city treasurer of Corinth, and here is his name cut into this ancient road. The bronze letters may be missing, but seeing his name—a fellow Christian, albeit from the first century—always has a peculiar effect on me.

"It's as though this ordinary man, only once mentioned in the Bible, brings the ancient city of Corinth back to life. Standing here by his name, I can imagine the workers building this road, no doubt on a deadline, and I can see the dedication ceremonies here with Erastus standing nearby."

Anne Marie visualized the scene as he described it: the ancient Corinthians wearing *chitons*, the scribes taking careful notes about the occasion, Erastus's name on their scrolls. After a while she joined the others taking pictures. Being here by this first century road with an ordinary citizen's name on it made the past more real to her, too.

Jon strolled around the ancient ruins, then gravitated to her side as everyone gathered near Efrem in the afternoon light.

"After leaving Athens, the apostle Paul came to Corinth," Efrem began. "Here Paul met a Jew named Aquila, who had recently arrived with his wife, Priscilla. They'd been expelled from Italy because of Caesar's order to deport Jews from Rome. They were tentmakers, as was Paul, and he lived and worked with them."

Standing in the sunshine and warm afternoon breeze, Anne Marie tried to visualize how life must have been among the tentmakers in the ancient city.

"Paul spoke in the synagogue every Sabbath, trying to convince both Jews and Greeks about Jesus," Efrem continued. "When Silas and Timothy came from Macedonia, Paul spent all of his time preaching the message that Jesus was the Messiah. When the Jews opposed him and blasphemed against Jesus, Paul said, 'If you are lost, it's your own responsibility. From now on I will preach to the Gentiles.'"

Anne Marie was drawn to Efrem's words. There was something about being here where the apostle had once been—perhaps even standing on the place where he'd stood—that made his life in the first century events quite real, too.

"Crispus, the leader of the synagogue, and his household believed in the Lord and were baptized, as were many of the others here in ancient Corinth," Efrem said. "One night Paul had a dream in which the Lord told him, 'Do not be afraid! Continue speaking out! Do not quit! I am with you and no one will be able to harm you. Many in this city are my people.' So Paul stayed here the next year and a half, teaching the Word of God."

When it was time for the group to leave for their buses, Anne Marie felt a wrenching sadness. It was more than the fact that she'd likely never come here again. Her fellow travelers seemed to move on with the same reluctance.

On the bus ride back to the ship, everyone was quiet in the afternoon heat, and some of the older people dozed in their seats. The guide occasionally pointed out sights in the countryside, then in the suburbs, for the most part adding to her earlier comments since they were returning on the same road.

"Tired?" Jon looked down at Anne Marie, his expression kind.

Anne Marie nodded, not really wanting to talk. On the

other hand, if she slept, she might miss something. Now was the time to gather memories.

It was pleasant to view the scenery from the height of the bus window, riding almost regally above traffic and pedestrians with the warm breeze blowing through the open windows. Whenever she glanced at Jon, she sensed his interest, but was determined not to encourage it.

The *Golden Isle,* tied up on the blue bay in Piraeus, was a magnificent and welcoming sight after the hot afternoon. *The first thing I need is a cool drink, then a shower,* Anne Marie thought as the bus stopped in the dockside parking lot.

Jon stepped off the bus behind her. "Let me buy you another lemonade. There's an outside refreshment bar on the Promenade Deck."

She was thirsty again and it would be interesting to see the daytime view of Piraeus from the deck. "Thank you, I'll take you up on it. But this time I'm buying."

Minutes later, walking out on the ship's Promenade Deck, she turned from the glorious view of the bay and hillsides of Piraeus to find Lila Thornton watching them from a chaise lounge near the swimming pool. Lila wore a minuscule white bikini that hid little of her glowing tan; her red hair, sleeked back, cascaded from a high and dramatic fall. Averill was nowhere in sight.

Anne Marie smiled at Lila, but the redhead simply stared at them.

Near-sighted, Anne Marie guessed. It occurred to her, too, that it was rare to find a tan redhead; Lila's hair was likely the color of her choice.

Anne Marie followed Jon to a white wooden table and chairs in the shade near the bar. It felt wonderful to sit out of the sun with the soft Mediterranean breeze blowing across her bare arms, but after a while she sensed that Lila was watching them with interest.

Settling back while Jon ordered lemonades and pistachio nuts, Anne Marie decided to ignore the woman's presence.

The waiter left. "Do you know that redhead?" Jon asked. "The one putting on her sunglasses."

"Slightly. I met her last night. She and her husband are friends of Alex. Business acquaintances, I take it."

Jon looked curious, and she went on. "Her husband's an archaeology enthusiast and interested in a new find in Athens. Medieval walls, I think." It occurred to her that with a wife who looked like Lila in a bikini, Averill would do better to pay more attention to her and less to medieval walls.

Jon turned back and sat with Anne Marie in companionable silence until the waiter brought their drinks and snacks. It seemed that all young Greek men, even the waiter, reminded her of Alex. It was well past siesta time, and she supposed Alex was at his desk with last-minute business.

Sipping the cool lemonade, she absently watched Jon tear open the bag of unshelled nuts.

"I made a study of the experts in Constitution Square opening these pistachios the first time I was here," he chuckled. Demonstrating, he pried one nut apart, then used the empty shell as a lever to open another for her.

Anne Marie smiled, accepting the nut. "Thank you. It's a pleasure to be served a pistachio nut by a student of the art."

Lila was suddenly standing beside them. "May I join the fun?" She asked her German accent more pronounced than it was last night.

"Of course." Anne Marie was taken by surprise. Uncomfortably introducing Lila to Jon, she wished that the woman had at least slipped a pool cover-up over her skimpy bikini.

Jon rose quickly, acknowledging the introduction. He helped Lila into another chair at their table.

Lila protested, "I can only stay one minute, but I had to meet your very handsome friend."

She turned to Jon. "Do you come from Nebraska, too?"

Jon smiled. "No, Southern California."

"Really, California? And you are on the religious tour?"

"Yes, I am." Jon sat back, awaiting her reaction.

"I must tell you, I find so many handsome men come from California," Lila said. "Perhaps more than from anywhere else in the world. There must be something about the air or the weather..."

Had she made a study of it? Anne Marie thought with annoyance, then watched Lila charm Jon most effectively.

When the waiter stopped by to inquire whether Lila wanted a drink, she laughed, "Why not? A small glass of white wine, but not *retsina*. I do not drink *retsina*."

Anne Marie finished her lemonade as she listened to Lila discuss Greek *retsina* wine, which apparently meant it was strong with the taste of resins. She finished with, "It is too Greek for me. I prefer the French or Italian white wines."

Anne Marie gathered up her sweater and handbag, and rose from the table. "Excuse me, but I have to get back to the cabin now."

Lila remarked, "I was...how do you say...lonesome for company. I do hope I haven't chased you away."

"Of course not," Anne Marie replied. "We only stopped to quench our thirst."

Jon rose to his feet. "See you at dinner?"

"No, but thank you. I'm having dinner in Athens."

Without awaiting his reaction, she hurried away, then was a trifle embarrassed because she hadn't paid for their lemonades as promised. Next time...if there was one.

Just as she reached for the deck door she overheard Lila suggest to Jon, "Perhaps you'll join us tonight in Athens?"

"Thank you," she heard Jon reply. "Only if I won't intrude."

Lila laughed. "But of course you won't! I know I speak for all of us. You would be most welcome. One can never have too many handsome men on hand, can one?"

Anne Marie hurried into the ship's corridor, more than annoyed now. It would be bad enough sharing Alex with Lila and Averill Thornton tonight. But now Jon's unnerving gaze would be on her and Alex, too.

CHAPTER

Five

At seven-thirty, Anne Marie settled onto a luxurious velvet sofa in the elegantly appointed Mediterranean Lounge to await Alex's arrival. She was only vaguely aware of the artistry of the jazz pianist.

Alex's note had said to meet him at exactly this moment. But where was he?

Fifteen minutes later, Alex arrived with Lila, smiling and lifting his hands apologetically. He rolled his eyes hopelessly toward Lila. "Some women have no concept of time!"

Anne Marie met his appraising gaze. "I'm here."

"Thank goodness."

Jon strode in behind them with an unreadable smile. Both men were stunning in dark suits, and Lila wore a simple, black backless silk dress that must have cost a fortune. Her auburn hair was swept back and pinned into an elegant twist.

Anne Marie was glad she'd brushed her thick hair out into soft waves and curls. She'd found the turquoise georgette dress with its touches of gold on sale in Santa Rosita. Metallic threads streaked through the blouse and the full Indian print skirt. A soft ruffle fell from the scooped neckline, and luxuriant diaphanous sleeves ended in ruffles at her wrists. Aunt Sylvia's gold charm bracelet and gold hoop earrings added to the gypsy effect.

"You look absolutely beautiful, Anne Marie Gardene," Alex smiled appreciatively. "A blond gypsy?"

"Do you think so?" She was pleased by his reaction. "I'll have to admit that I've never before worn anything like it."

"You do look wonderful," Jon said quietly.

"It's an amusing dress— " Lila began.

Anne Marie interrupted before the woman could continue. "Exactly what I thought. But these colors make me feel light-hearted. Just the thing for tonight!" Ordinarily, she'd have chosen something more sophisticated for the evening, but tonight she wanted to feel carefree. This last year she'd borne enough problems and responsibilities for a lifetime. Moreover, she suspected that Lila would find any dress she chose to be "amusing."

Lila simply stared at her without expression.

Anne Marie wanted to change the subject. "Where's Averill?"

"Exhausted by climbing about the ruins. I invited your handsome friend, Jon, instead. I hope you don't mind." Lila rested her hand on the sleeve of Jon's jacket, and he looked somewhat uncomfortable.

"Of course not," Anne Marie managed. She smiled at Jon, then turned to Alex, grateful that he offered his arm.

"Lila's very persuasive," Jon said.

Alex laughed his hearty Greek laugh. "Now that is the greatest understatement I've heard in a long time!"

Apparently Averill didn't mind his wife going out with other men, Anne Marie thought. An unusual relationship.

The sea air was pleasantly warm as they walked down the gangway to the silver Andropoulos limousine. On the wharf, Anne Marie glanced back at their white ship silhouetted against the night sky. She would not let Lila destroy this evening.

As the chauffeur came out to help them in, Alex looked at Jon. When he spoke his tone was stiff. "We'd better put our long-legged American friend in the middle seat."

Surely he's not jealous of Jon's height, Anne Marie thought. Alex was quite tall for a Greek, only three or four inches shorter than Jon.

Alex helped her into the back seat, then climbed in beside her, his white smile wide. "Tonight, my blond gypsy, we shall dance like never before!"

She laughed. "Olé!"

He laughed with her. "No, not like in Spain or Mexico! Did I tell you about when I ran with the bulls in Spain?"

"No! You most certainly didn't."

"In Pamplona, one summer vacation between my years at Harvard. My mother was not pleased."

"I can imagine. I've seen the casualties on TV. Last year two young men were killed."

"It's a risk, but risks keep life more interesting." He settled back into the seat, his dark eyes never leaving her face.

"Is that your philosophy, taking risks to keep life interesting?"

He laughed again. "Part of it."

She smiled and shook her head at him. "Exactly how you played soccer back in Nebraska—running wildly, dodging unexpectedly, kicking for impossible goals—taking risks every minute."

"A good way to play the game of life," he said. Anne Marie did not reply

During the drive to Athens, the conversation moved among the four of them, and Anne Marie wished she could have Alex to herself. Still, she was the one who sat at Alex's side, and occasionally he patted her hand as they discussed the sights and the evening ahead. The plaka, the old town near the Acropolis, was, as he'd mentioned this morning, the place in

Athens for tourists to shop, but the authentic Greek dishes and dancing had moved out to the suburbs.

"I'm afraid I won't know how to do the dances," Anne Marie said after a time. "I should have warned you this morning. I vaguely remember square dances and bits of an Irish jig from dance classes, but we didn't have Greek dances."

Alex chuckled softly. "I'm sure I can teach you." His words held such a sensuous undertone that she blushed. He laughed and finally turned his attention to Lila and Jon in the seat in front of them, regaling them with stories about their surroundings.

Watching him, Anne Marie enjoyed his exuberance. It showed even in the set of his chin; he was determined to live life to the fullest on his terms. And there was an elegance about him, too—an elegance that almost stretched to arrogance as he sat back casually in his dark blue mohair suit and white silk shirt. He knew exactly who he was and where he was going.

Moving closer, she smiled up at him.

He raised a dark eyebrow and slipped a proprietary arm around her shoulders. "My beautiful blond gypsy."

My dark, handsome Greek, she thought.

The chauffeur drove them to Pandrosou Street, and Anne Marie and the others waited at the curb while Alex made arrangements with the driver.

The car pulled away and Alex turned again to Anne Marie. "I knew you would like to see this area. All the tourists come here."

"They certainly seem to," she agreed as they moved into the crowded streets. Anne Marie's high heeled sandal twisted on a cobblestone, and Alex caught her, slipping a steadying arm around her waist.

"Cobbled streets are no place for high heels, but I'm glad now you wore them. Are you all right?"

She nodded quickly. "Yes. I'm fine." In fact, she was grateful for the excuse for him to hold her as they made their way through the throngs of tourists on the sidewalks.

The narrow shops held thousands of old books, jumbles of antique brass and copper, buckets of old coins, and other curiosities. She thought that Lila might make a caustic remark about being thrust among common tourists, but a shop window featuring great brass ship's lanterns caught her eye.

"Exactly what I've been wanting for our London terrace!" Lila headed straight into the shop.

Alex sighed indulgently. "Lila is a shopper extraordinaire. With her in tow, it will take us hours to make the short walk through the plaka."

"It's fine with me," Anne Marie replied happily. The shops were like none she'd ever seen. Even if she didn't buy a thing, it was an adventure to browse through the antiques and curiosities—and maybe find things for her kindergartners.

Jon seemed equally pleased, his attention caught by a bucket of old Greek coins, and Anne Marie recalled that he'd collected coins as a boy. In fact, Aunt Sylvia had often added coins to his collection from her travels.

They followed leisurely in Lila's wake from one quaint shop to another until she'd purchased five large antique brass lanterns and arranged for their shipment to London.

Lila frowned at Anne Marie as they left the shop. "Aren't you going to buy anything else? The prices are very good here."

Anne Marie had already imagined how lovely a ship's brass lantern would look on Aunt Sylvia's patio, but she'd settled instead for post cards of the Acropolis and a few inexpensive coins that supposedly dated back to Roman times for her students.

She smiled at Lila. "Afraid I can't afford a lantern."

"Oh?" Lila responded with a sharp glance. "What you need is a rich husband!"

Alex gave a laugh. "Aha! We shall have to tell Averill what you are advising!"

"It's no secret to him," Lila sniffed, then turning, she took Jon's arm with a flourish. He laughed as if he had no objection at all.

Slowly they made their way through the maze of narrow back streets with tavernas, some built against the rock wall at the base of the Acropolis. A sense of unreality overcame Anne Marie again; it seemed impossible that she could be here in the plaka with Alex, but the cobblestones underfoot provided assurance that this wasn't a daydream.

Later, the Andropoulos limousine met them on the main street, and they drove to the suburbs for Alex's favorite restaurant. At length, he announced, "Ah, here we are. We used to have tavernas like this in the plaka until the tourists took over." He raised a hand to stop any protest. "Not that we don't appreciate tourist money, of course."

The driver helped them from the limo, and Alex escorted them through a gate, then out to an old open-air taverna where the smells of good food seemed to have permeated the centuries-old walls.

"Alex!" the owner called out and embraced him heartily.

Alex introduced everyone as the owner led them to a table near the outdoor dance floor. The waiters held out the chairs and shook Alex's hand as if he were a favored guest as well as an old friend.

Alex settled next to Anne Marie at their table. Jon and Lila sat across from them. "Do you like it?" Alex asked. "It's a place the tourists can't find."

"It's wonderful, Alex. I love the tiny lights in the trees." She thought she'd be happy anywhere with him, but this was especially delightful.

"Yes, in Greek tavernas it's Christmas year around."

The lights in the sprawling tree limbs gave the setting a romantic glow, and lively Greek music swirled around them as the musicians toured the garden.

"It's a long way from rock music."

"Thank goodness! I prefer this. In fact, I love it!"

From the glint in his eyes, she suspected he knew that she loved more than the music and surroundings—that she loved being with him. He appeared as pleased as she felt, then turned at the waiter's approach with the menus.

She accepted a menu, all of it written in Greek.

Alex glanced at Anne Marie as she tried to read the list of dishes. "What would you like?"

"You order for me, please. No wine, though."

"No wine? They have more than retsina to offer here. In fact, they have a good variety."

"It's just that I...I prefer lemonade."

Alex raised his brows. "You Christian girls—you're hard to understand."

She opened her mouth to protest, but Jon quickly spoke up. "I'd like roast lamb, and a lemonade."

Alex laughed. "Maybe I should have said, 'You Americans!' Wine is such a part of Greek culture. Are you sure you want lemonade?"

Jonathan grinned. "I'm sure."

Anne Marie thought she'd explain once and for all. "I don't like alcohol. The truth is, it gives me headaches."

Alex drew a breath of acceptance. "Well, then at least I won't have a drunken young woman on my hands."

She decided not to mention that there'd been so much drunkenness at college that she'd vowed never to be a part of it. Her freshman roommate had been so caught up in the drinking scene that she'd been date-raped her first month there, and she was only one of many whose lives had been damaged by drinking.

As for her being a Christian, she thought that Alex must have assumed it even though she'd told him she'd inherited her ticket and was not a pilgrim. Maybe it was because she'd attended church as a girl when he lived with them in Nebraska. She sometimes wondered about her exact status herself. But she didn't attend church now, and at her parents' church, everyone assumed they were believers because they came to Sunday morning services. She tried to be a good person.

Alex leaned forward, speaking to all of them. "Jon guessed right. The roast lamb here is exceptional. Even better than on the ship, though you can't quote me on that."

Minutes later, he ordered their meals in Greek, and Anne Marie understood his rueful tone of voice when he ordered the two lemonades.

Across the table, Lila sat back smugly, exhaling smoke from her cigarette. Her upturned lips gave every appearance of enjoying Anne Marie's lack of sophistication.

The busboy arrived quickly with black olives, dolmades, a tomato and lettuce salad with feta cheese, and the best mousakka she had ever tasted.

While they ate, Alex called out something in Greek to the musicians as they neared their table, singing a folk song.

He turned to assess Anne Marie's reaction. "Wonderful, too?"

"It's hearty and lively, just like you Greeks." Her words brought on his exuberant laugh.

After a while the musicians moved to a corner of the dance floor while Anne Marie and the others ate. For dessert, there was honeyed baklava, a pastry she'd ordered at home when she had thought of him.

Someone shouted, and Greek men and women started toward the dance floor.

"Ah. Now the dancing begins." Alex leaned back in his chair, smiling expectantly.

Instead of couples dancing together, the men and women formed a circle on the dance floor, holding corners of white handkerchiefs between them. As the rhythmic music began, the circle of dancers moved by a series of intricate steps in one direction, then the other.

Suddenly a woman let go of the handkerchiefs and danced to the center of the circle to perform a few solo steps, then returned to pirouette under the upraised arm of her partner. As she resumed her place, the adjoining man danced out alone toward the center of the circle. The rest of the dancers performed intricate steps together.

Anne Marie leaned toward Alex. "How do they know when to do the solos?"

"It's an old Greek dance."

Lila smiled up at him meaningfully. "Again, Greeks just know?"

He laughed. "Yes, there are some things in life that Greeks just seem to know from birth, don't you think so, Lila?"

Anne Marie tried to ignore the provocative undercurrents in their tones and turned her attention to the last bites of her baklava.

The lively music and dancing swept through the taverna with only occasional intermissions. "The dances all tell stories," Alex explained. "This one, the *Kalamatianos,* is from a legend about the Turkish occupation when a village of unguarded women committed suicide rather than fall into the hands of the invaders."

Watching the dancers under the dim courtyard lights, Anne Marie felt estranged from Alex, alien to his culture. Even later, during less calamitous dances, the foreign sounds of the music hung like a curtain between them. The dancers' rhythm went on and on, and it was as if they'd bridged time to their ancient tribal days. Yet the music was not wild, and the continuous flow of the dance was beautiful to watch. The thumping of the dancers' feet sounded like soft drums in the sensuous night air.

After the busboy had cleared the table, the dancers pulled Alex to the floor to join them, and Anne Marie was taken aback at how easily he shed his sophisticated persona and became a common Greek dancing the centuries-old folk dances. Concentrating on the intricate steps, he lost himself in the performance.

"The Greeks learn the dances nearly as soon as they learn to walk." Lila gazed at Anne Marie with a knowing smile. "Life, as you must see, is different in the Middle East."

Anne Marie looked at her evenly. "I see Greece as a part of Europe."

Lila smiled. "As Alex says all too often, Greece is Greece."

Anne Marie didn't answer and, across the table from her, Jon was equally quiet as he watched the entertainment.

The evening ended with circle dancing around the entire courtyard. Alex hurried to the table and laughingly pulled them to their feet. "Everyone dance! Come! Everyone dance!" His voice was exuberant.

Anne Marie tried to pick up the intricate steps, and after a while Alex urged her onto the dance floor in a solo performance. Caught up in the excitement, she moved forward. Her steps seemed vaguely like a folk dance she'd learned in school; everyone cheered her on.

Her breathless words were directed to Jon as she returned to the circle. "The Greeks must be the most tactful people on earth!"

"You mean you didn't know what you were doing?" Jon laughed. "You danced like a gypsy!"

"You are next, Jon." Alex seemed certain that Jon would turn down the challenge.

"Forward!" Jon surprised them all by moving forward with great agility; for a man his height, he acquitted himself surprisingly well.

"Good job!" Anne Marie called out as he danced back. "The Greeks aren't the only ones who can dance!"

Alex laughed. "Now it's Lila's turn."

When Lila danced forward in her slithery black dress, it was clear she was no newcomer to Greek folk dancing. The men cheered at her sensuous rendition of the dance, and she went on, encouraging them.

After the dancing ended and everyone returned to their tables, Alex caught Anne Marie lightly by the shoulder. "Are you having a good time, my Nebraska cornflower?" He leaned close, his dark eyes sparkling.

"Marvelous," she whispered. "Even more than marvelous."

He looked as if he might try to drop a kiss on her forehead. "I am glad that you've come here—more glad than words can say."

On the way to the ship, in the back seat of the Andropoulos limousine, he sat with his arm draped casually around her. In the middle seat, behind the glassed partition separating them from the chauffeur, Jon and Lila gazed out the window, admiring the nighttime views.

Anne Marie looked past Alex to the Acropolis, bathed an eerie white in the moonlight. High above the city, it stood like an awesome temple on an otherworldly outcropping of land. She was so caught up in the sight that Alex took her by surprise as he reached for her shoulders.

Just then Jon turned toward them. "It's been a wonderful evening, Alex. We would never have had such an authentic Greek evening without you. Thank you for showing us around."

"My pleasure." Alex let out what seemed to be an exasperated sigh, and settled back into the seat.

Anne Marie turned again to the ancient view of the Acropolis out the window. Its unearthly whiteness transformed it into an apparition from an ancient planet, an apparition from ages past. How did it affect modern Athenians like Alex to see the Acropolis at night? Did they think of their ancient gods? Did they make secret vows and sacrifices?

As they neared the ship, Alex's arm remained around her shoulders. But the eeriness of the Acropolis and the memory of the folk dances made her apprehensive.

She sighed deeply, glancing at him in the darkness of the limo. Despite their cultural differences, she knew something momentous was building between them.

A short time later, the four entered the ship's elevator and turned as the doors closed. Jon, moving to stand near Anne Marie, said pointedly, "I can see Anne Marie to her cabin. It's next to mine."

"Oh?" Alex asked as the elevator started upward. He looked at her, his dark eyes glimmering with suspicion.

"Most of our tour group is clustered in nearby cabins," she explained hurriedly.

Lila laughed. "I'm sure that our friend Jon can be left in charge, Alex. He strikes me as a trustworthy sort. Very upstanding and reliable."

Alex gave Lila an odd look, which she returned with an ironic smile. "I could use some assistance to my cabin since I'm on your deck," she said. "Averill may not get around like he once did, but he does like to know that I'm being well cared for."

"Yes, of course, you'll be well cared for," Alex replied evenly. "Aren't you always?"

Lila replied with another sardonic smile.

Why such deference for Lila and Averill? Anne Marie wondered. Was Averill's bank a major lender for the Andropoulos shipping line? Was it mainly a business friendship?

Seconds later, the elevator had stopped on the Aegean Deck, and she and Jon stepped off. "Thank you for a lovely evening," she called back to Alex.

"My pleasure," he replied with a nod.

"And good night, Lila," she added.

"Good night," Lila said, then turned with a broad smile at Alex as the elevator door closed.

Jon remained quiet as they walked through the corridor to their cabins. Arriving at cabin thirty-three, he stopped. "Do you have your key?"

"Yes, of course."

She fumbled in her evening bag, hoping he wasn't waiting for her to hand it to him. Finding the key, she unlocked the door. As she looked up before slipping into her cabin, Jon's blue eyes held hers with a hopeful expression.

"Good night, Anne Marie." His voice held a hint of huskiness.

She managed a soft "Good night, Jon," then closed the cabin door far too quickly.

What was that all about? she wondered in the dimly lit cabin. What was happening?

CHAPTER

Six

Awakening, Anne Marie heard the muffled throb of engines, then felt the *Golden Isle* begin to move slowly. She opened her eyes to a shaft of gray light slanting through the porthole above her bed.

"Anne Marie," Beth whispered. "You awake?"

"Almost," she answered groggily. "We didn't get in until after two."

"It must be five o'clock," Beth said. "The ship's leaving for Delphi."

The cruise portion of the trip is underway, Anne Marie thought with peaceful pleasure. She rolled over drowsily, too tired to get up, yet wanting to see everything, too. "Would you wake me just before we go through the canal?"

"I'll order a wake-up call for you just before we go through," Beth promised. "I'll do it right now so I don't forget. And I'll try to be quiet."

Anne Marie fell back asleep.

When the wake-up call came at seven o'clock, she vaguely recalled their conversation.

"Good morning, Miss Gardene," said the Greek voice on the

phone. "Seven o'clock. We shall soon go through the Corinthian Canal. Have a fine day."

"Thank you."

Her cabinmate's bed was empty; she was probably on deck with Efrem to watch as they sailed along the Greek coast. Anne Marie regretted not seeing it, but it would be impossible to see everything on the cruise. She closed her eyes, wanting to spend a few minutes reliving the memorable evening at the plaka and the taverna.

Hurry! she chided herself suddenly. This was no time for daydreaming. If she didn't get going, she'd miss one of the highlights of the trip.

Ten minutes later, she had pulled on a white polo shirt, tan shorts, and white sandals and brushed her hair into a short ponytail. In the mirror, she looked surprisingly fresh and rested, but too plainly dressed. She found her colorful wooden animals necklace and slipped it on. Far better. Lila would surely disapprove of the necklace, but kindergartners loved it.

She grabbed the cabin key and rushed out into the corridor, greeting a couple from the Santa Rosita group who were also hurrying out to see the canal crossing.

Out on the Promenade Deck, she found a crowd of passengers watching the proceedings in the sunshine. The *Golden Isle* had come to a complete stop, and a tugboat maneuvered into place at the bow to guide them through the narrow channel cut through the brown and green hillside.

"Over here, Anne Marie!" Jon called out through the crowd near the railing. He stood with Beth and Efrem, obviously pleased to see her.

She couldn't help smiling back as she made her way to them through the crowd of passengers. "Good morning, all."

"Isn't it a great morning?" Jon asked, allowing her to squeeze past him to stand with Beth at the railing. "I was afraid you might miss the excitement."

Anne Marie laughed. "Not me!"

"Some claim it's more interesting than the Panama Canal," Beth remarked, watching the canal-crossing procedures with them.

"Have you been here before?" Anne Marie asked Efrem, knowing he'd made several earlier trips to Corinth on church Holy Land tours.

"My first time through the canal, too," he replied with enthusiasm. "I've always seen it from up on the bridge like we did yesterday."

Anne Marie was aware of Jon watching her, and determined to discourage him, she turned her attention to the Greek countryside. The land on either side of the canal was a golden brown, and dark green trees shaded the nearby village and dotted the distant hillsides. A warm breeze brushed the back of her neck under her ponytail.

The *Golden Isle* began to move toward the canal, then suddenly lurched forward, throwing passengers off-balance. "Oh!" she cried out with others, losing her balance.

Jon caught her by the shoulders to steady her. "Gotcha!"

She laughed uneasily. "Thanks!"

"My pleasure." His eyes met hers for a moment before he moved away. "Any time you need catching, keep me in mind."

Instead of replying, she gave him a small smile and quickly glanced back at the decks above them.

No sign of Alex.

As the ship entered the narrow channel, Anne Marie edged away from Jon at the rail. Surely the look in his eyes when he caught her wasn't merely the concern of an old friend. She tried not to think about it as they moved through the narrow canal, the *Golden Isle*'s sides seeming just inches from the fearsome stone walls rising on either side.

"Here goes our ship's white paint!" Beth predicted.

"For the captain's sake and the sailors' sakes, let's hope not!" Efrem laughed. "It would not only mar the ship, but their careers as well."

Small school children in their uniforms ambled along, eyeing the passengers from a path so close to the ship that they could have jumped aboard.

"I wonder what they think of us," Jon mused. "We passengers act like children out on an exciting outing, and the children look as somber as world-weary adults."

Beth laughed, and Anne Marie agreed with his thinking.

When the *Golden Isle* emerged into the Aegean Sea unscathed, another cruise ship was waiting on the side to enter the canal. At first the other ship seemed a startling illusion because their vision had become so narrowed by the slow and lengthy passage.

"Well, now we've been through the Corinthian Canal, another man-made marvel," Jon said, a touch of irony in his voice.

"But a *spectacular* marvel," Efrem countered.

"There's something special about passing through, too," Anne Marie said. "Maybe it's the canal's place in history. Or that it's located in such an historic area..."

"Or the romance of it?" Efrem asked.

"Yes, I suppose it is the romance of this place that makes it so exciting," she agreed.

Jon shot another curious look at her. "Romance does make the world far more interesting."

No comment! she decided.

The morning's excitement over, passengers headed to the dining rooms or toward the back of the Promenade Deck where a continental breakfast was being served.

"Where would you like to eat?" Jon asked Anne Marie.

Beth and Efrem had already decided on the dining room, since they'd been out since dawn and were famished. Despite their invitation, Anne Marie answered, "Outside, I think. I want to see this famous Greek coastline."

Jon looked pleased as they headed for the buffet. With red and blue chaise lounges fanned out around the pool, the Promenade Deck was such a tempting sight that nearly every seat was taken.

She smiled up at him. "Shall I try to find us two chaises?"

"Great. And I'll grab some fresh orange juice. I remember your penchant for it. What else would you like?"

"Surprise me."

"I'll try." Smiling, he made his way to the line of passengers at the buffet tables.

Anne Marie found two empty chaises against the deck railing. Before sitting, she glanced up to the higher decks for Alex, then in disappointment, back over the railing. Behind her the wake flared out, its white water sparkling like a rush of diamonds, then smoothing again as if the ship had never passed through. The sapphire Aegean was a dazzling sight. It occurred to her that not only was this breathtakingly beautiful moment passing, but her entire life seemed to be hurtling by just as quickly.

Sudden tears filled her eyes.

Why was it that she was so often on the verge of tears since Aunt Sylvia's death? A bleak sadness flooded through her, and she quickly turned away from the wake to sit down, trying to shake her mood.

At length, Jon returned, bearing a yellow plastic tray with glasses of orange juice, cups of steaming coffee, freshly-baked croissants, and packets of butter and jam.

Her voice was a little too bright. "Croissants must be the surprise."

He chuckled. "Not very surprising."

They devoured their breakfasts as they watched the rugged Greek coast pass by. The modern city of Corinth gleamed in the distance beyond a wide stretch of sapphire sea, and yesterday's visit to ancient Corinth already seemed long ago.

Her mind wandered to the morning breakfasts she and Jon had shared together under the great pepper tree on Aunt Sylvia's patio, and her old resentment resurfaced. What possible excuse could he have had for not coming home for the memorial service? What possible excuse?

He frowned at her in concern. "Something wrong?"

"Nothing worth ruining the views for."

Gazing at the distant coastline, she thought again that her emotions had been more unpredictable and turbulent lately. She'd have to keep them under control.

After a while John remarked, "There's a talk about Delphi at ten in the Macedonian Lounge."

"Yes, I'd like to hear it." She added abruptly, "I suppose you've already been there."

"No, I've never been to Delphi."

Regretting her curtness, she softened her voice. "All I remember about Delphi is that most of the Mediterranean world flocked to the oracle there for advice." Even as she spoke, she glanced around again for Alex, not really expecting him to be about at nine-thirty in the morning. At any rate, he could see the coastlines of Greece any time he wished.

She and Jon sat silently in the warm morning sunshine, watching their fellow passengers and trying to locate on their cruise maps the islands they passed until it was time for the Delphi talk.

Just before ten o'clock, in the Macedonian Lounge, Beth and Efrem waved them over from across the crowd. The auditorium-sized room was already so jammed that people were beginning to stand against the walls.

"Thank goodness you saved us seats." Anne Marie said, and sat down on a small couch next to Beth and Efrem's. Jon settled beside her, his arm resting on the back of the couch. She edged away uncomfortably even though he sat a reasonable distance from her.

"Are you venturing out into the pagan world of Delphi?" he teased Efrem.

Efrem laughed. "The apostle Paul did, and it was a completely pagan world then. It wasn't just a matter of the simple people being committed to gods and goddesses. Even emperors looked into the entrails of oxen for answers to national affairs."

Beth lifted an eyebrow and smiled. "See how much easier it is for you to spread the gospel now."

"I don't know about that!" Efrem answered with a laugh. "It strikes me that simple pagans may have been easier to reach than the so-called intellectuals we have now. Worldly knowledge, no matter how distorted, seems to close man's ears to the truth."

Jon speculated, "Maybe it's because gaining knowledge is such an expensive pursuit nowadays that people don't want their intellectual investments challenged."

Anne Marie knew she certainly didn't like having her body of knowledge questioned. It stirred up too many complications, even doubts. It was far easier to believe in whatever she'd already accepted as true—far easier than rocking the intellectual boat.

At the front of the room a young man wearing a *Golden Isle* T-shirt tapped the microphone for attention, ending the crowd's buzz of conversation.

"Welcome to our first ports-of-call talk," the young man said, then introduced himself as the cruise director. "I'd like to introduce the staff."

Everyone from the captain to the vivacious American girl who conducted exercise classes spoke at the microphone for a minute or two. It was a young crowd to run a ship, except for Captain Papadakis, who had graying sideburns.

Finally the cruise director turned his attention to the ports of call. "Delphi is one of the most impressive archaeological sites on the Greek mainland," he began.

"It was the political, economic, and religious center of much of the Mediterranean world for ten centuries. Kings, princes, and pilgrims came from as far away as Persia and Egypt to offer homage and treasures for the oracle's answers to anything from national policy to personal problems."

Anne Marie marveled that she was really going there. She looked around the room for Alex, but there was no sign of him. No sign of Lila or Averill, either.

The director continued, "The oracle, who was said to have the voice of Apollo, was really a succession of young maidens who chewed hallucinogenic laurel leaves and moaned oh-so-mystically above the volcanic vapors."

The audience chuckled, and the tour director grinned. "Priests—who were usually advised what the supplicants' problems might be—were ready with enigmatic answers to any questions. When the mighty offered treasures like gold, silver, or ivory to Apollo, you can be certain that the oracle's performances were very good indeed."

After the talk, the crowd dispersed down the corridors for an eleven-thirty lunch since the ship would dock at Itea, the port for Delphi, at one o'clock.

"Dining room or the Promenade Deck for the buffet?" Jon asked Anne Marie at the elevators.

"Actually, I think I'll go back to the cabin for a bit," she replied, hoping there might be a message from Alex.

Beth looked at Jon. "We're eating out on the Promenade

Deck. Won't you join me and Efrem?"

She smiled at Anne Marie. "We'll hold a place for you in the buffet line in case you change your mind."

Was her cabinmate playing matchmaker? Anne Marie wondered as she took the lead in the corridor. Maybe not. Maybe Beth was merely trying to smooth matters over because it was natural for her to do so. Or maybe because it seemed more appropriate for her and Efrem to be among others.

The elevator door was opening, and Anne Marie said, "See you in a while." She got on and gave them a friendly wave. On the Aegean Deck, she hurried down the corridor. Surely Alex had left a message for her.

But when she opened the cabin door, the phone's message light was dark. No note under the door, no blinking light on the phone. The only good news was that the beds had been made and everything was immaculate.

She decided that Alex might be having lunch in his own cabin or with the captain; after all, he was checking out the ship. She quickly freshened up, then brushed her hair and retied it with a white ribbon.

Arriving outside on the Promenade Deck, she noted the buffet lines stretched halfway along each side of the ship.

"Here we are, Anne Marie!" Beth called out. She and Efrem smiled a welcome, but Jon wore his sunglasses now, and it was impossible to read his expression. Only ten or eleven passengers stood in front of them, a great long line stretching behind.

Anne Marie spoke to a couple standing behind them. "Do you mind if I join my friends?"

"No sense in hurrying," the man said with a chuckle. "We're all in the same boat, and we're all going to get far too much to eat." His words reflected the relaxed air of the crowd.

Instead of worrying about Alex, Anne Marie turned her attention to the sumptuous buffet set up in the shade of the overhang. The aromas of fried chicken, Greek sausages, dolmades, fish, moussaka, and lamb dishes wafted from the enormous stainless steel serving dishes. There was also a salad bar as colorful as an artist's palette. Next to it were arrangements of cakes, pastries, cookies, and giant platters of fresh fruit.

"I can't decide," she said, then like everyone else, helped herself to bits of everything.

"You, too?" Jon asked ruefully as they stepped away from the buffet with their overladen plates.

"Me, too. I'll probably go home fat."

"I can't imagine that." He laughed, briefly meeting her eyes.

She quickly looked away, searching for Beth and Efrem. "There they are!"

Tray in hand, she wound her way through the crowd on the port side of the ship. She followed Beth and Efrem, who headed to a table shaded by the upper deck. Efrem took Beth's tray, and their eyes held lovingly.

"Are you sure you want company?" Anne Marie asked as Efrem held Beth's chair out for her to sit.

"We're more than sure." Efrem looked up with an embarrassed grin. "Just sit across the table from us. Maybe Jon will say grace."

Jon settled beside Anne Marie. "I'm honored, Efrem." He and the others bowed their heads, and Anne Marie felt compelled to follow suit.

"Our loving Father," Jon began. "We want to thank you for your love for us and for the beauty of your creation. You are the giver of so many good gifts, and you have been faithful to us all of our lives. We are grateful for all you are to us and for this food. In your Son's name we pray. Amen."

Tears welled in Anne Marie's eyes, and she blinked hard as she unloaded the dishes from her tray onto the table. *Toughen up,* she told herself. *Toughen up.*

Fortunately the breeze dried her tears and no one seemed to have noticed. Hearing Jon pray might have softened her heart, but it didn't mean she could forgive him.

As they ate lunch, she tried to join in the light-hearted conversation, though it didn't stop her from looking about occasionally for Alex.

Surely he would appear in time for the tour to Delphi. Surely he hadn't forgotten her now.

CHAPTER

Seven

At the small port of Itea, Anne Marie was halfway down the gangway before she saw Alex standing among the crowd on the dock. He waited with the Thorntons and, seeing her, beamed like the afternoon's dazzling sunshine.

He must not have realized she saw him amidst the crowd of disembarking passengers, for he called out over them, "Anne Marie, here!"

She waved and hurried down the gangway, excited about the afternoon trip to Delphi.

Alex grinned as she joined them. "Where were you, in the ship's hold?"

"Unfortunately on the wrong deck for the gangway," she admitted. "I'm afraid I don't quite have the disembarking procedure figured out yet. I thought we were leaving from the Ocean Deck."

Lila's lips curved into a superior smile, but Averill nodded pleasantly. "Nice to see you again, Anne Marie."

"And you," she answered. "I'm sorry to have kept all of you waiting."

In truth, no real arrangements had been made for her to

spend the afternoon with them, but they'd apparently expected her and had somehow disembarked quickly.

"No problem," Alex said. "The buses always keep everyone waiting anyhow." He caught her hand in his as they started down the dock for the tiny village.

Her heart leaped at his holding her hand so publicly. "You mean we're riding on a bus?"

Alex chuckled. "In these days of downsizing businesses, you didn't think our family kept a limousine and a driver in a little port like Itea?"

She shrugged. "You just don't strike me as a bus rider, but then neither do the people on the tour with Efrem Walcott. It seems that being a tourist changes one's standard of living—and not necessarily to the luxurious levels depicted in travel brochures!"

Alex gave a laugh. "You're learning quickly."

After a moment, he asked, "Tell me, what kind of a 'rider' do you see me as?"

"Ummm...let me think. I guess I see you as a luxury rider—private planes, great white yachts, maybe a personal space shuttle waiting on the liftoff pad."

He threw back his head in hearty laughter.

As usual, it was a pleasure to see him laugh.

"Come on." Still grinning, he pulled her hand. "Let's head for the village." They started through the crowd.

Lila spoke from behind them, her tone petulant. "You might have hired a village taxi."

"Lila, dear, you can stop playing the princess," Averill muttered to his wife.

"It will do you a world of good to ride the bus, Lila," Alex added. "It gives one the commoner's perspective."

"I have no wish to acquire the commoner's perspective," Lila sniffed. "There's nothing 'common' about me, and I see no reason to suffer anything 'common' in my life."

"My father always says never to let yourself get too far above the common man," Alex tossed back over his shoulder. "Once the air becomes too rarefied, one loses sight of how the world actually runs."

Lila smiled wryly. "I know more than enough about how the world runs." After a moment, she asked Anne Marie. "Where is your tall, handsome friend?"

"Jon?"

"Of course Jon."

"With the Santa Rosita group, I assume. They chartered their own buses so they can stay together."

Alex's amusement faded. "You're not involved with Jon, are you?"

"We're old friends. He was my aunt's attorney."

"But you're not romantically involved?"

Anne Marie felt uncomfortable. "Of course not." Perhaps she'd once been romantically interested in him, but he'd never reciprocated. He'd never so much as tried to hold her hand or kiss her. He'd only braided her hair.

"Sorry," Alex said softly. "It's just that I don't want to tread where I might make trouble."

Behind them, Lila laughed at something, but Anne Marie ignored her as they walked along the narrow dock. Alex had as much as admitted he was attracted to her—Anne Marie Gardene. "You won't make trouble."

"Good." He brought her hand to his lips and kissed it. "I'm so glad you're here. You put a whole new perspective on everything. You make the world shine like new."

"I do?"

He grinned. "You do."

It is a glorious day, she thought as they stepped off the dock and into the charming village of Itea. Two school girls watched them holding hands, and some elderly men in dark suits sat on the park benches, smiling at the group. Shops lined the waterfront street, and sleepy-eyed villagers rushed out racks of colorful clothing and carried out copperware to tempt the *Golden Isle*'s passengers, many of whom were already rummaging through the merchandise near their buses.

"It means a great deal to the small villages when our cruise ships arrive," Alex explained. "The Iteans have given up their afternoon naps. Our shipping line takes pride in bringing a bit of prosperity to the countryside."

"That's a side of you I haven't seen before—this sense of responsibility for your countrymen."

"You don't like it?"

"On the contrary. I'm proud of you, Alex. It is an attribute I've never witnessed in another man."

He gave an embarrassed laugh. "Come now, I'm sure you need to add to the Iteans' wealth."

"Let's see if I can."

She bought a floaty lavender shift with a flounce around the bottom, a floppy straw hat, and, for her students, postcards of a ship making its way through the Corinthian Canal. "How am I doing for the local economy?" She smiled up at him as she made her way to the cash register.

He laughed. "Fine for a beginning."

Back on the sidewalk, she plopped the floppy straw hat on her head, making him laugh again. Walking along, the two of them browsed through the clothing and souvenir shops on Itea's main street before it was time to board a tour bus.

She and Alex found a seat behind the Thorntons, and Anne Marie slid into the window seat behind Lila, trying to pretend the woman wasn't there. It was difficult, however, to disregard Lila gazing out the window with her self-possessed manner. Her luxuriant auburn hair was pulled back into a high fall again, and her flawless tan contrasted with her revealing black sundress.

Anne Marie considered her own sedate white T-shirt and tan shorts, and wished she'd worn something more appealing. Still, Alex seemed very interested in her. She glanced at him as the bus started off, and he gave her a satisfied smile.

The bus driver conferred with their guide—an elderly man, this time—then signaled with his arm out the open window before he drove the bus out onto the almost empty main street. Just beyond the village of Itea, olive groves covered the hillsides, and their guide quickly took over. "Olive oil is Greece's main export," the man said into his microphone.

"My Athens guide didn't tell me that," Anne Marie remarked mischievously to Alex, referring to his role. "I don't think he knows about the crops and such."

Alex grinned, slid his arm around her, and intoned in a serious tour guide voice, "During the harvest season, they put nets on the ground and the younger children climb up in the trees to shake the black olives from the tree limbs while the older children gather the olives from the nets. Green olives are more expensive here because they are still picked by hand, one by one."

"And how do you happen to know?" she inquired.

"I have cousins in the villages. As a boy, I often helped with the olive harvest."

"You?"

"Me," he admitted happily. "I am not all private planes and yachts and personal space shuttles. Besides, I like to shake trees."

"I'm not surprised at the tree shaking. You are a mover and shaker."

He laughed. "I hope so."

Once they were beyond the olive groves, the road curved

treacherously up the foothills. Despite Anne Marie hanging onto the seat grip, the bus's turns shifted her and Alex against each other. He voiced no objections, nor did she.

"Notice the views." He gazed out the window.

"I am."

Her open window framed magnificent vistas of mountains and the sparkling Aegean Sea, and the road's switchbacks took them higher and higher until the olive groves below looked like green seas. She sighed happily, caught up in the majestic beauty and Alex's nearness.

She turned to him and found him watching her intently.

"When you look at me like that," he said huskily, "I know that 'someday' has indeed come." He pulled her closer.

Caught up in the majestic beauty and Alex's nearness, Anne Marie thought that she'd never been so happy, that she could ride on like this with him forever.

In the flower-bedecked village of Delphi, their tour guide pointed out its delightful hotels, restaurants, and shops and told about summer performances of the old Greek plays in the ancient amphitheater they would see higher on the hillside.

"I ski here in the winter," Alex said. "How I would like to bring you, Anne Marie."

"And how I would love to come here, with you!"

"We'll count on it this winter."

"I'll do it." Perhaps she should stay on after the cruise even though his family hadn't asked her; Alex would work it out. Perhaps his family had left it to his discretion.

From time to time Lila darted glances back at them, and Anne Marie pretended not to notice.

They got off the bus near Delphi's museum, where majestic gray mountains surrounded them like great stone cathedrals. It was easy to imagine why the ancient Greeks might think the god Apollo lived here among the mountains.

"First, the museum. You must see the statuary that wasn't carted off to other countries." Alex's voice was laced with a note of bitterness.

The Thortons caught up with them, Averill out of breath.

"I didn't realize you were such an expert guide, Alex," Lila said sarcastically.

He gave her a half-smile.

"Save enough time for the ruins," Averill advised. "These tours rush one along too much."

"And how many times have you already seen Delphi, Averill?" Alex asked as the men took out the entry tickets.

Averill grinned. "I've lost count. But it can never be too many for me."

Anne Marie thought that Lila looked disinterested in the surroundings as they waited to enter the museum, but once inside, Lila started happily for the gift shop and Averill went his own way into the ultra-modern museum.

Alex guided Anne Marie through the throngs of tourists and the maze of rooms that displayed bronze and marble statues as well as bas-reliefs removed from the ancient temples and treasuries. The starkly modern museum set off the ancient pieces to great advantage.

"You must see the famous charioteer statue," he said.

When they entered the room that featured the dramatically placed bronze statue of the charioteer, it nearly took her breath away. Oxidized through the centuries to a soft gray-green, the life-sized statue of the aristocratic young Greek chariot racer seemed real, an epochal athlete caught in that moment when he triumphantly presented himself to the cheering crowd. His almond-shaped eyes, made of white enamel and brown stone, looked so real that he might have been...Alex...yes, Alex, but thousands of years ago.

The thought of it thrilled her. She moved on reluctantly as

he escorted her through the museum, determined that she see as much as possible in the short time remaining.

Outside there were groups of tourists with their guides speaking French, German, English, and Japanese. As she and Alex started down the Sacred Way of Delphi, Anne Marie marveled that they walked on the same marble that had been trod by kings and commoners through the centuries.

Alex smiled into her eyes. "It's a pleasure to show you about. We Greeks have seen ruins for so many years that we've lost our enthusiasm about the ancients. Some even find the constant excavations into antiquity a bore."

"I can't believe it. How could anyone not be intrigued?"

"There are always those who take no interest in others, only in what affects them directly. It's the same everywhere."

"I'm glad you're not one of them," she told him.

"You bring back my enthusiasm." He took her arm as they continued past the ruins.

An English-speaking guide said, "The ancients believed the first temple was made of intertwined laurel branches. The second temple was supposedly made of beeswax and wings, the third of bronze, and the fourth built by legendary architects known from the 'Homeric Hymn to Apollo.' The nave was divided into two parts; in the front there was an altar of Poseidon and statues of the Fates..."

Alex guided her forward as the guide continued, "Few people were allowed into the second part of the nave which contained a gold statue of Apollo."

It struck Anne Marie that throughout history people had searched for a higher power. Sometimes she wondered about God; he seemed so terribly far away, yet some people claimed they had a close relationship with him through Christ. After hearing Jon pray, she supposed that he must. But *how* could one even go about having a relationship with God?

Alex stopped for her to take pictures where the volcanic vapors were said to have inspired the fabled Oracle of Delphi. Then it was time to hurry on, to climb up the rocky hillside to the chalky marble amphitheater.

In the distance she saw Beth, Efrem, and Jon, although they didn't see her. They and the others on the "footsteps of the apostle Paul" journey were making a pilgrimage in honor of God, much as the ancients had come to Delphi to honor the old Greek gods—and to hear from the famous oracle, of course.

What must the Santa Rosita group think of these ancient beliefs? What was it Efrem had quoted from the apostle Paul on Mars Hill? *Men of Athens, I see that you are quite religious. While I walked about, I saw your many altars. One of them especially interested me. Its inscription said, "To the Unknown God."* Then he'd gone on to tell them about God.

Alex led the way up the rocky path, and they emerged high on the hill by the enormous stadium of the ancient Greeks. Catching her breath, Anne Marie marveled at the vastness of the stadium with its tiers of stone benches.

"Can't you see the ancient athletes coming out onto the field to the roar of the crowd?" Alex asked.

She nodded. "And you're one of them?"

He looked pleased. "Yes, sometimes I pretend I'm one of them."

Taking pictures, she noticed that the few others who'd climbed this far had already left. She and Alex were alone in the awesome mountainside stadium. "I can't bear to go." She knew they should rush to the bus.

"I can't either," Alex said with a slow smile. He took her hand and raised it to his lips.

She thought that they might have been two people from antiquity, upon whom the warm breezes blew and the sun shone.

Alex smiled down at her, seeming to read her thoughts. "It's as if the ancient fates destined this moment just for us." He kissed her fingertips again.

Ancient fates? The thought made her suddenly uncomfortable, and she pulled her hand away.

She drew in a deep breath as phrases from Jon's prayer came back to her. "Our loving Father...thank you for your love for us...You are the giver of so many gifts...You have been faithful..." And she remembered Aunt Sylvia's last words—that Anne Marie would come to know how much God loved her, that his love was forgiving, unchanging, eternal.

Anne Marie lifted her eyes heavenward, considering such a personal God. But he seemed as far away as Alex's ancient fates. She wondered briefly at the sadness that seemed to have cast a shadow on the day. But wanting nothing to ruin her time with Alex, she brushed the thoughts aside and again smiled up at him.

His dark eyes held hers. Then he took her hand and guided her back down the hill.

CHAPTER

Eight

Anne Marie and Alex ran down the hillside of Delphi holding hands. "Don't worry," he told her, "the bus driver will wait. Now this is what Greeks call living." He looked up at the brilliant sky and the vistas around them with such excitement, she thought he might break into dance. His exuberance was infectious—intoxicating.

"Some Americans would be in agreement." Her words made him chuckle.

"Have you ever had such an afternoon?"

She shook her head, trying not to dwell on the thoughts she'd had on the hill. "No. And you?"

"Never," he replied. "And I've been to Delphi plenty of times. I didn't know it could be even more wonderful than hearing from the oracle."

This time she laughed with him.

When they finally reached the parking lot and their tour bus, its motor was running. Obviously, they'd delayed everyone on the bus.

Climbing on board, Anne Marie tried to ignore the driver's annoyance, though his expression quickly turned pleasant as

Alex rattled off something in Greek to him. It sounded like advice to be gracious to tourists—and it appeared that the driver had belatedly realized who Alex was.

The bus doors flapped shut immediately, and the driver swung the steering wheel around so quickly that Anne Marie barely caught her balance as the bus pulled out onto the road.

She pretended not to notice Lila's curious stare as she and Alex hurried down the aisle toward the back of the bus. Averill, like several others, lay back against his seat fast asleep in the warmth of the afternoon sun after the exertion of climbing through the ruins.

Laughing and out of breath, Alex settled beside Anne Marie in a seat near the back of the bus. "We made it! Didn't I say not to worry?"

Anne Marie smiled and nodded. She wondered if he cared for her as much as she cared for him. It crossed her mind that he might be contemplating a fast fling. She quickly dismissed the possibility, though, oddly, she felt a need to conceal her feelings for him. He was likely the kind of man whom a woman should keep guessing.

She sat back and tried to catch her breath. Finally, she became aware of the warm breeze blowing through the windows.

After a while, Alex reached for her hand, and she let him hold it. The dark hair on his firmly muscled arm entranced her; he was far more masculine now than he'd been as a teenager. As she looked up at him, he pulled her close, trying to snatch a kiss.

She ducked it. "Not here!"

"We're in the back of the bus," he whispered. "If not here, then where?"

She put a finger to her lips. "Shhhhh!"

"And when, Miss Teacher?"

She shrugged, looking up at him coquettishly.

"Now," he said, trying to trap her against the window. "Everyone's sleeping. Look at them...how do you say it...'sawing wood.'"

"Alex!"

"Come here, woman, this is Alex, the risk taker."

She pressed him away, almost laughing aloud. "This is Anne Marie, who is only learning to take risks again."

Their teasing helped her forget the shadowed moments on the hill. She tried to recapture the earlier feelings of euphoria, surrounded by his nearly overwhelming presence and the glorious Greek countryside.

When they climbed off the bus in Itea, Alex turned to her. "The captain has invited us to sit at his table for dinner."

"Tonight? Isn't it the captain's welcoming gala?"

"It is. I accepted for you, of course."

Her heart leaped with excitement. "It sounds lovely. But I didn't bring a terribly formal dress. Kindergarten teachers rarely attend such occasions."

"We'll take care of that easily."

In the village of Itea, they had half an hour for shopping, and after the bus let them off, they quickly made their way down the main street.

"Here," Alex guided her toward a shop. "I intend to buy you the perfect dress for tonight."

"No, Alex, I can't let you buy me...clothing."

"And why not?"

Heat rushed to her cheeks. "My Aunt Sylvia always said never to let a man buy me clothing."

"She sounds old-fashioned."

Anne Marie let out a sigh. "I suppose she was."

"And prudish?"

She nodded. "Maybe a little." But even her more liberal

mother had said, "If you let a man buy you clothing, he begins to think that he owns the body under it."

Alex looked at her with interest. "Hasn't a man ever bought you clothing?"

"Never. I suppose the occasion hasn't presented itself. I'm not the type—"

He interrupted. "I know just what you should wear tonight. Something exquisite and...yes...restrained."

"Alex, you can't..."

Ignoring her protests, he headed for a rack of long silk dresses and pulled out a white dress, its short sleeves and bodice appliquéed with white satin thread. The dress was indeed exquisite—and modest.

"You'll be a golden goddess in it," he said, holding it against her. He stood back slightly, assessing the effect. "You must wear your hair down, too."

She glanced at the price tag. "It's too expensive."

"I can afford to be generous. Just look at all that your family did for me. Consider it a small return on their investment."

The shop owner spoke to him in Greek, and he translated, "She says it was appliquéed by the village's best artisan. It's a one-in-the-world dress."

"Alex...no."

"For me?" he pleaded. "In memory of your parents?"

She drew a breath. "When you put it that way, I'll let you win."

"Good."

He turned to the shop owner with his credit card.

"What if the dress doesn't fit?" Anne Marie asked.

Alex smiled. "With a Harvard education, don't you think I can at least estimate your size? You are slightly taller and far more curvy than when you were a teenager."

Heat rushed to her face again, and she was suddenly aware

that other tourists in the shop had been listening. To her surprise, one older woman nodded and winked. Anne Marie turned away from her while Alex completed the transaction.

Fortunately the dress was modest, Anne Marie reminded herself as they left the shop. Still, her mother's and aunt's admonitions rang in her head.

Walking up the dock with the other returning passengers, it occurred to her they hadn't seen the Thorntons in some time. "Where are Lila and Averill?"

"Aboard ship, I suspect," Alex answered. "Averill tires easily since his heart attack. And Lila is, at times, a devoted wife to him. Especially when it suits her purposes."

"Tell me about Lila."

Alex raised his brows thoughtfully. "She grew up poor but determined to be rich. Averill is not her first elderly husband, and I doubt that he'll be her last."

"I see. I shouldn't have asked." It occurred to her that a woman such as Lila would have to harden her heart against hurt, particularly what others thought.

They watched another white cruise ship sail into the small harbor. Anne Marie wanted to change the subject. "More income for the villagers."

"Yes," Alex replied. "It's a second class line. I don't like to see it flying the Greek flag."

She glanced at the blue and white striped flag with its white cross in the upper left-hand corner. "Second class—a *Greek* ship?" Her tone was teasing.

"Even the Greeks are not all perfect," he answered with a chuckle. "As far as I know, the only one on earth who was perfect is the One your tour group reveres."

"One?" She tilted her head, though she thought she knew what he meant.

"The Hebrew—Jesus."

She nodded. "Yes...that's what I've been told, as well." The mention of the Santa Rosita group again took the sunlight out of her day. What would they think of Alex buying her this dress? It was clearly visible through the thin plastic bag, and even more obvious, Alex carried it over an arm.

As they walked up the gangway, the *Golden Isle* blasted its five-minute warning, the low sound filling the harbor and village of Itea. In the distance, straggling shoppers rushed toward the dock, their arms laden with bags and packages.

In the ship's elevator, Alex said, "We eat at the seven-thirty seating, although I can't imagine how civilized people can have an appetite by then. Meet me for a drink at seven in the Ionian Lounge."

"Fine," she replied, a bit put off by his commanding manner. "I expect you like your siesta and dinner at ten."

"I do," he replied, his dark eyes dancing. He handed her the bag with the dress. "Ionian Lounge. Seven o'clock."

"I'll be there."

Stepping out of the elevator with the white dress, Anne Marie was glad there'd be time for a short rest. Exciting as their excursion to Delphi had been, it had also been tiring.

When she opened the cabin door, the almost funereal smell of the red roses assailed her. Then she saw Beth on her bed with her back to the door, and Anne Marie quickly slipped the new dress into her closet. Turning, she realized her roommate was crying.

"Beth, what's wrong?"

Beth shook her head. "Nothing...just nothing!" she blurted, then shook with sudden sobs again.

"It must be *something* to hurt you like this. You're usually so cheerful. If someone had told me you cried, I'd have said, 'Beth Stillman is definitely not a crier.'"

Beth's sobs subsided. "Oh, I cry all right."

"Is it Efrem?" Anne Marie asked, though she couldn't imagine Efrem Walcott upsetting Beth like this. She hurried around to sit on the bed facing Beth.

Her roommate sniffled, her tears still flowing. "Please, don't tell him I've been crying!"

"Of course I won't," Anne Marie promised. "I won't tell anyone, for that matter." Disconcerted, she felt uncertain about leaving the cabin or putting her arm around Beth as she would her kindergartners. She decided to do neither. "Would it make you feel better to talk?"

Beth caught her breath. "It's just that people sometimes don't think before they speak."

"I hope it's not something I've said."

Beth shook her head dolefully.

"Has someone been dreadful to you?"

"No. If people were dreadful, I could probably handle it far better." Beth looked up at her. "It was just little Mrs. Mitchell across the corridor, who wouldn't want to hurt a soul. Efrem kissed me at the door. It was a wonderful spontaneous kiss, and no one was out there. Then Mrs. Mitchell opened her door. When we saw her, she asked ever so sweetly, 'Why don't you two lovebirds get married? It would make me so happy. There's nothing like love.'"

"What did you say?"

"Oh, Efrem laughed it off somehow and I hurried in here. Believe it or not, it's the first time he's ever kissed me, and to be caught in the middle of it...and then have someone mention marriage when his wife's only been dead for nine months. It nearly bowled me over."

"Bad timing."

Beth nodded. "With him being a minister, it's very difficult. Last month one of the elders walked into Efrem's office, and I was standing behind his chair and giving him a neck rub. Poor

Efrem was tense and exhausted. With my nursing background, it wasn't the intimate gesture the elderly man seemed to think."

"I can imagine," Anne Marie said.

"Then Efrem left a Post-it on my desk, reminding me of what time he'd pick me up for dinner—a rare occasion—and a deacon saw it. As if that wasn't enough, a page from my spiritual journey journal fell out, and Mrs. Nathan came across it in the church parking lot. I'd written about how I felt God had led me to Efrem and how much I cared about him, not only as a spiritual leader, but as a man."

"Was she upset?"

"Upset, amazed, curious. You name it. But I don't think she told anyone. She's not a gossip. Actually, nothing terrible has come of our dating, but it's difficult to be haunted by what people in such a staid church might think."

"Does it really matter that much?"

"Not to most people maybe, but it does to me and to Efrem. The Bible says we're not to do anything that might cause our brother to stumble. No matter how we feel about each other, we don't want to give an appearance of impropriety."

Anne Marie's heart ached for her. "You do have to consider matters differently than most people."

"We do."

Beth stood up and began to pace between their beds. "I love him. He's the finest, most upright person I've ever met. He's honest and decent and responsible—everything in a man that I've always hoped for."

"You've never been married?"

"No. And it seems I've been single forever," Beth answered. "I've prayed for years for God to send someone right for me. And now at age thirty-nine when I'd almost given up, he did." She drew a shaky breath. "I suppose we'll just have to wait and wait."

"How long?" Anne Marie asked.

"I don't know. Maybe forever."

Beth paced quietly, then added, "After hoping for so many years, I'm just impatient. And for all I know, I'm assuming too much, and he doesn't even want to marry again. Living with an invalid for so many years can't have made for an easy marriage. And I'd like to have a home and children before it's too late. I don't even know how he feels about it, only that we're never to give the impression of impropriety."

"Does he have children?" Anne Marie asked.

Beth shook her head. "His wife had multiple sclerosis from early on in their marriage. There were endless complications. At least having children opposed to his remarriage isn't one of our problems." Beth stopped abruptly. "I'm sorry. I shouldn't unload my frustrations on you. Mrs. Mitchell's comment unnerved me. There are people in the congregation who loved his wife dearly and would probably never...accept him remarrying. At least not for a long time."

"Did you know his wife?"

"No, I never met her."

She added, "I lived in northern California most of my life. I worked as a nurse for years. After Mom died, it was time for a radical change. I moved to Santa Rosita and took the church job six months ago. I fell in love with Efrem fast, but it's taken more time on his part. For a man who's so enthusiastic and exuberant, he's very cautious."

"I'm sorry, Beth."

Beth looked at her gratefully before shaking her head at herself. "I've waited so long. And now to think I had to fall in love with a widowed minister only to face this business of...never giving an impression of impropriety!"

"Did he say that?"

Beth shook her head. "We both agreed on it the very first

time he asked me out for dinner. And believe me, we did not dine anywhere near Santa Rosita!"

Anne Marie's heart ached for Beth. "You two are so right together. I love seeing how he looks at you so adoringly."

"It's obvious?"

Anne Marie nodded. "It's obvious, and a joy to see. I can't understand how it can be so much trouble."

"I suppose it's because there's an older congregation involved." Beth stopped and blew her nose. "Some have attended the church for decades. And there've been so many scandals about ministers elsewhere lately, we don't want to add to the distrust."

She managed a wry smile. "Anyhow, he's the most wonderful man who's ever come into my life. I just hope he doesn't disappear. I've always told the Lord that if I were to marry, to please send someone who'd be the spiritual leader in our family. In that category, not one of the men I ever dated was even a remote possibility."

"What are you going to do?"

Beth rose to her feet. "Put the whole matter back in the Lord's hands where it belonged in the first place." Her sweet expression held determination. She grabbed her shower cap from the dressing table and headed for the bathroom. "God will let me know what to do. It's only when I take matters back on my shoulders like this that it hurts." She sighed. "If only I could always remember that!"

Tears welled in Anne Marie's eyes. She wasn't sure how she might handle Beth's situation, but she did admire her roommate's concern for others' faith.

She glanced at her watch. Time to rest for a few moments, she thought and pulled off her shoes. She lay down on her bed and considered what to wear with the exquisite white silk dress. Perhaps Aunt Sylvia's gold necklace, earrings, and bracelet. As for shoes, her white heels would have to do.

Five minutes later, Beth emerged from the bathroom wearing a white towel wrapped around her body and a glorious smile on her face. "Sorry I wept all over you."

"No problem. You look fine now."

"I've put it all back into God's hands and don't intend to take it back. Now tell me about your day in Delphi with your handsome friend, Alex."

Anne Marie gave her a wry smile. "You're not the only one in a muddle. I hope that's comforting to you."

"And exciting! I do hope he's an honorable man."

"I hope so, too," Anne Marie answered, attempting to hide her apprehension. "At any rate, I've known him for a long, long time."

After Beth left, Anne Marie marveled at how deftly her roommate had turned the subject from her personal despair to Anne Marie's day at Delphi. As she dressed, she realized she'd been so caught up in Beth's problem that the captain's gala dinner had paled by comparison.

Dressed, she examined herself in the mirror.

Her blond hair fell in thick waves and ended with soft curls curling under just past her ears; her eyes were bluer against the tan she'd acquired during the last two days. She hoped Alex would be pleased with her appearance, especially with the white appliquéed silk dress clinging lightly to her body. The dress was so lovely that she no longer felt quite so guilty about accepting it from him. After all, times had changed since Mother and Aunt Sylvia's days.

Minutes before seven o'clock, she stepped into the Ionian Lounge. Passengers wearing evening dresses and white dinner jackets or tuxedos sat at the tables and the bar, imparting a sophisticated atmosphere. Several couples at tables and even those dancing to the soft music turned to admire her.

Alex strode toward her from the bar, reaching out with both hands. "A Greek goddess. Exactly as I thought."

Smiling, she let him take her hands. "A blond Greek?"

"Some historians speculate that the ancient Greeks were blond and blue-eyed. It's usually refuted by the rest of us."

She gave a laugh. "It is difficult to believe." She decided not to say that, if anything, he was the stunning one in his white dinner jacket, white silk shirt, black bow tie, and black slacks.

"The dress fits beautifully," he said with an approving glance. "It's even more beautiful than I suspected."

"Thank you again, Alex." From the corner of her eye, she saw people were staring. "Let's sit down."

He laughed. "Let everyone stare. It's not often they are treated to Greek goddesses nowadays."

The lounge manager hurried to escort them through the open doors to an outdoor table. The barman arrived at their table so quickly and bowed with such respect that Anne Marie had to hide her smile.

"What will you have?" Alex asked her.

"Tonic water, please."

His brown eyes widened with concern. "Are you sure? Perhaps some white wine?"

"No, thank you."

"Ah, yes, you mentioned it gives you headaches."

"Yes, and I don't enjoy headaches."

While Alex ordered her a tonic water and white wine for himself, Anne Marie noticed Jon sitting with Rena and Reynold Williamson two tables away. Jon looked up at her and smiled.

"Your friend, Jon." Alex paused significantly.

For once, she offered no comment.

Alex added, "He's an attractive fellow."

She nodded. "Yes, he is. I'm sure he's much sought after by young women."

The glint of jealousy in Alex's eyes surprised her. He reached for her hand and held it on the table as if to publicly lay claim to her.

It was only a few minutes before the dinner bells pealed out over the loudspeakers. "Ladies and gentlemen," the suave voice announced. "Dinner is now served for those at the second seating. We wish you bon appétit."

"I'm starved," Anne Marie admitted. "Again!"

"I am too." he chuckled. "The cruise industry could save a fortune by eliminating the bells. It's like Pavlov's reflex conditioning. The bells ring and the passengers salivate."

She gave a laugh. "Then no one could complain about how much weight they gained on their last cruise, which is such good advertising!"

"Yes, I suppose it is."

No one spoke on the crowded elevator to the dining room deck, but she noticed other women staring at Alex as if thinking, *the heir to the Andropoulos shipping fortune.* She felt certain he knew and quietly enjoyed their admiration.

At the dining room entrance, she looked up at Alex, and his brown eyes held hers for a disturbing moment. She was nearly unaware of the maitre d's nod to her. He then turned to Alex. "*Kirie* Andropoulos."

"Captain's table, please," Alex said, nodding curtly.

"Of course, sir. This way, if you please."

Making her way through the festive dining room, Anne Marie noted the colorful flags hanging from the ceiling and, below, a sea of beautifully set tables with white damask cloths and silver vases with varicolored flowers. An air of expectancy filled the room as diners settled at their round tables, which were hovered over solicitously by an array of captains, waiters, and busboys.

The other diners were already seated at the captain's table, most seeming as pleased as Anne Marie to be there. She noticed that only Alex, Lila, and Averill accepted the honor as their due.

The men rose as introductions were made. Captain Papadakis kissed Anne Marie's hand with a continental flare. "Good evening, Miss Gardene," he said. "I am charmed to have you at my table this evening."

His eyes glowed with admiration, then darted to Alex, who smiled back enigmatically. Certainly the captain would be curious about her since Alex was heir to the Andropoulos shipping lines, she realized as she was seated.

At the captain's left sat an elderly widow, dripping with jewelry; two middle-aged couples occupied the next seats at the round table; then Averill Thornton and Lila, who unfortunately sat on Alex's right. Lila, as always, looked spectacular, tonight in a satiny green strapless dress.

Their waiter, elegant in black suit and tie, presented great embossed menus. Anne Marie puzzled over the selections: oysters, caviar, shrimp, lobster, steak, prime rib, fish, roast lamb, and other dishes.

When Alex asked what she would have, she shook her head hopelessly. "Too much to choose from."

"Better we were ancient Greeks content with olives, bread, and an occasional roasted lamb."

"I sometimes think so myself," Captain Papadakis joined in amiably. At this distance, he looked slightly older than he had that morning when he had been introduced at the port-of-call talk. Behind him, a server filled their goblets with tinkling ice-water, while another presented a tray of freshly baked rolls whose fragrance filled the air.

Anne Marie made her decision. "Roast lamb again. I enjoyed it so much last night."

"And the Greeks will all be ordering steak and prime rib,"

Alex chuckled. "How we welcome a change from our ever-present lamb and shish kebabs."

After the waiter had taken their orders, the conversation turned to travel. Lila and Averill had often cruised on the *Golden Isle* and her sister ships, and they'd recently spent a month in Australia. Apparently they traveled constantly, possibly to keep from being bored, Anne Marie speculated. Everyone else at the table seemed widely traveled, too.

"And you, Miss Gardene?" the captain asked. "Do you enjoy traveling?"

"Yes," she replied, "although this is my first real trip out of my country." She decided the jaunt to Tiajuana with Jon and his friends scarcely counted.

"She is our innocent," Alex said.

Anne Marie noticed Lila's condescending expression.

But Captain Papadakis's expression was kind. "You will be seeing many countries for a first trip abroad. I always envy my passengers who are on their first voyage. The first voyage is usually one's most exciting trip, the one that's remembered for a lifetime."

Anne Marie flashed him a grateful smile.

"It's a bit like the first time one falls in love, I suppose," he added. "First love is also so memorable."

She felt another flood of warmth rising to her face and was certain she hadn't blushed so much in her life as she had recently. Fortunately, the bejeweled woman moved the discussion to the ship's ports of call.

Within minutes the first course was served. Anne Marie turned to her hors d'oeuvre: a tiny dish of red and black caviar served with toast tips and sprigs of watercress. She watched the others, then squeezed a serrated lemon half over the caviar. Best not to tell them this was her first time for caviar, too. She tasted it uncertainly and found she enjoyed its piquant flavor.

"I understand you're a teacher, Miss Gardene," the captain commented.

"Yes, I teach kindergarten."

The captain raised an eyebrow at her and then Alex. "Much like Princess Diana of England once did, though that didn't turn out so well in the end."

Alex merely smiled.

"It's not every day that I have the pleasure of sitting beside a kindergarten teacher," the captain continued. "Tell me, how did you decide to teach such young and *active* children?"

She laughed softly. "Do you mean *unruly?*"

The captain nodded. "I would never attempt it. It's my guess that most of us at this table would never dream of working with a room full of children that age every day. Do tell us why you chose it."

"I suppose it's because of their innocence. Small children are still open and loving—and full of energy, too, of course."

"I see. A bit like young lambs bursting out of their pens and gamboling out into the world."

"An apt comparison."

The waiter moved between them to serve their salads, and Anne Marie wondered why people frequently questioned why she taught small children. Perhaps it was so she could borrow the children until she had her own. And because small children responded so openly to love.

The dinner progressed with elegantly-served dishes and wines to accompany each course. Anne Marie found little to add to the conversations about travel, particularly with Lila holding forth. Still, it was entertaining to hear others' travel stories. It also was exciting to see Alex so often glancing appreciatively toward her.

When they rose from the table, he caught her hand in his. "A walk about the deck? Then we can catch the evening show."

"That sounds lovely. Just what I need."

She backed away slightly at the smell of alcohol on his breath and noticed that Lila and Averill were leaving by the other dining room door. Thank goodness Alex hadn't suggested joining them. "You know what a fresh air person I am," she added. "Pure country girl."

"I didn't think you'd enjoy a smoky, noisy bar."

She smiled her appreciation as Alex opened the door to the Promenade Deck. "Look how magnificent it is out here."

Night had fallen and the ship sailed through the darkness for the island of Crete. Protected from the cool wind, the leeward side of the deck was crowded, and there were no deck stewards to find them a special seat.

She and Alex strolled to the railing, admiring the sliver of a moon, the stars high above, and the inky black sea all around them. How far away from the world they seemed here in the dim light. Yet the velvety blackness also imparted the sense of sailing into the unknown, much as her life felt like lately.

Alex slipped an arm around her waist. "You look stunning in the starlight. I had no idea that you would grow up to be such a beauty or I might have sent for you years ago."

"You might have *sent* for me!" she returned with a touch of indignation. Some of her more feminist friends at home would be appalled at the statement. She smiled, lifting an eyebrow. "One doesn't send for American women anymore!"

"So I hear," he replied, amused. "Now they send for the man! But a true man still likes to do the pursuing."

For a moment she let him draw her closer, then thought she heard Jon's voice. Turning, she saw him step out onto the deck with people from the Santa Rosita tour group. She removed Alex's hand from her waist.

He asked curtly, "Shall we go down to see the show? Lila and Averill are to hold seats for us in the Macedonian Lounge."

She preferred to stay out in the fresh air, but Alex looked annoyed, even in the dim light. She decided it was best to avoid Jon's scrutiny, too.

"Yes, let's go."

Beth and Efrem were at the deck door, just stepping outside and laughing about something, and they exchanged greetings with them.

After the door closed, Alex said, "Your roommate and the minister seem to enjoy themselves."

"Yes," Anne Marie answered. She wondered what Alex might think about Beth and Efrem traveling together and added, "Beth is a lovely person."

"She strikes me as hopelessly naive."

"Naive?"

He gave a quiet laugh. "I'm sometimes doubtful about priests and ministers, especially about their so-called 'morality' or 'purity.'"

She didn't appreciate his insinuation. "From everything I see and hear, Efrem Walcott strikes me as truly moral," she replied defensively. "Beth is too."

She suspected Alex had been about to say something more disparaging about ministers, then decided against it.

The show had begun when they entered the darkened Macedonian Lounge. On stage, the ship's combo filled the room with a vaguely familiar tune. Colorful streamers and balloons hung from the ceiling near the stage. How different the lounge had looked this morning when it served as the auditorium for the port-of-call talk she'd attended with Jon!

"There they are." Alex spotted Lila and Averill seated near the stage. "Leave it to them to get the best seats in the room."

The lounge manager rushed through the crowd to Alex, determined to escort them, and Anne Marie followed him through the lively audience to an empty sofa reserved for them beside the Thorntons, just below center stage.

As marvelous as it was to sit so close, she'd have preferred other seats just to be alone with Alex. Settling onto the sofa, Alex turned toward the Thorntons. "How did you manage these?"

"Simple," Lila replied with an artful smile. "We told them we're part of the Andropoulos party."

Alex laughed.

"Why not?" Averill inquired. "Without bankers, there would be no cruise industry. Rank has its privileges."

On stage, the tour director strode to the microphone. "Welcome to our Captain's Gala Night," he said over the music. "We begin the evening with the most beautiful dancers this side of the Acropolis—the *Golden Isle* showgirls!"

Anne Marie sat back uncomfortably as the scantily clad dancers paraded on stage and kicked their way through a cancan number. Something about the performance was demeaning to both the dancers and to the women in the audience, she thought. It was especially embarrassing to sit right below them.

She darted a glance at Alex, who watched them with an appreciative smile. She felt a surge of anger.

When the dance ended and the audience applauded, Alex turned to Averill. "Not exactly Paris, is it?"

Averill laughed. "Not in the least."

"Nothing is like Paris," Lila stated.

The waiter interrupted to take their drink orders. "Just tonic water, please," Anne Marie said despite Alex's frown.

"Double scotch," he said.

He'd already drunk a lot of wine, she thought, though he appeared unaffected by it.

He glanced at her. "What's wrong, my Nebraska cornflower? You're not jealous of dancers who aren't half as beautiful as you?"

She raised her chin defensively.

He leaned over and whispered, his breath warm in her hair, "You are the most delectable woman in the entire room."

"Now, Alex..."

He laughed.

A hypnotist started his act on the stage, but she scarcely noticed. Alex was the one who hypnotized her, the one who held her heart in his hands.

She watched him throw back his head and roar with laughter at the antics of the hypnotized passengers, and she recalled that back in Nebraska even her family had called it his "hearty Greek laugh." Oddly, she also recalled a Sunday school teacher's admonition to stay away from hypnotism, horoscopes, tarot cards, and related matters. She definitely did not wish to be a hypnotist's subject, though she was unsure why she felt so strongly about it.

The evening's featured attraction was a famous blond singer from the '50s, and her sultry voice filled the Macedonian Lounge with songs of love. It softened her heart, and Anne Marie thought she could never care for a man more than Alex.

The waiter made his way to them again and again, taking orders for more drinks.

"Alex, should you?" Anne Marie finally ventured after his third round.

His dark eyes glittered. "Are you trying to tell me what I should do?"

"Of course not," she answered quickly, worried at the anger in his voice. "I'm sorry if I...I'm sorry."

He nodded somewhat reluctantly, and she felt relieved.

When the show ended, he led her through the crowd, his arm around her. Lila and Averill were far behind. "Let's go upstairs and look at the moonlight again."

In the elevator, the uneasy silence of strangers hung about them. When they stepped out onto the Ionion Deck, she assumed they would go to the Ionian Lounge. Perhaps there was a deck there, too, for seeing the moonlight. Alex would know, and she didn't know her way around this deck at all.

They stopped at a cabin door, and Alex took out his key.

Her heart pounded with sudden alarm. "Where are we going?"

"Into my cabin, where else?" His voice was as smooth as honey. "We can see the moonlight from my balcony."

"I...I didn't know the ship had balconies."

"A few on this deck."

She backed away as he unlocked the door. "No, Alex, I don't think it's a good idea."

"And if I do?" he inquired. "After all, we're adults now. Don't you think it's high time we act like it?"

"Please...no...please don't ruin everything!"

He took her arm forcefully. "If you love me, you'll come in with me."

It was such an old line that she pulled away. "How could you, Alex? How could you even think this of me? I've given you the wrong impression."

"Come now. Surely you're not still that little innocent from Nebraska?"

"I am, Alex. Believe it or not, I am. No matter what society says, I'm still old-fashioned enough to believe in love."

"But that's precisely what I want, too."

She pulled away from him. "I said love, not lust, Alex!"

"Don't tell me your friend Jon—"

She interrupted before he could go on. "Stop it, Alex! Jon's never...never tried anything like this. I'm not what you think!"

Turning, she fled down the corridor, half-hoping he'd pursue her and say it was a misunderstanding, that they could go on as before, simply falling in love. A cabin door slammed, and when she glanced back, there was no sign of him.

Waiting for the elevator, her hands trembled. She choked back a burst of tears. On the elevator, people stared, and she bit down on her lips, trying to control her emotions. If only she hadn't let Alex buy this dress for her!

But it was far more than the dress. Alex assumed that American women—and likely other women—were all available to him. Their relationship was over, ended, and an agony of loneliness and heartsickness assailed her.

When she stepped into her cabin, she was glad Beth was out. As it was, the reek of fading roses gagged her. She plopped the bouquet of red roses out in the corridor, as if the angry gesture could forever end everything between her and Alex.

Tossing in bed most of the night, she dreamed intermittently of Lila Thornton. "You fool!" the redhead shook her finger at Anne Marie. "You had a real chance at Alex Andropoulos and gave it up for your prudish morals."

At nine o'clock the next morning, a knock sounded at the cabin door. Anne Marie blinked groggily. No sign of Beth. She slipped out of bed and pulled on her robe. Opening the door, she found the room steward standing in the corridor with a bouquet of pink roses for her. Accepting them with trepidation, she closed the door and tore the white card from its envelope.

I'll never understand Christian women.

Good-bye and best wishes,

Alex

Oh, Alex! her heart cried.

She hurt so much that no tears fell. She could only set the bouquet of pink roses on the coffee table and quickly turn away. She'd dispose of them in the corridor later. No more reminders of Alex. As for him thinking she was a Christian? She let out a deep sigh; that idea she refused even to think about.

At one-thirty she stood alone and heartbroken at the railing of the *Golden Isle,* watching their arrival at Heraklion, Crete. She'd spent most of the morning rereading the brochures, unwilling to get the book from her cabin. She wouldn't even be going ashore if she hadn't accepted money from a fifth-grade teacher friend to buy a piece of Minoan art.

In the distance, Mount Juktas resembled the profile of a sleeping man, or as the ancient Cretans said, the sleeping god, Zeus. She thought nothing of the seaplane waiting alongside the dock until she caught sight of Alex hurrying down the gangway with his briefcase, an attendant carrying his other luggage. As he headed for the seaplane, her spirits plummeted even lower.

"Andropoulos." A crewman nearby said the name to another, then continued in Greek about Athens.

She backed away from the railing, thinking she'd never hurt so terribly. All of these years she'd dreamed of Alex. All of it for nothing. No one seemed to notice her anguish. The other passengers hurried toward the gangway, intent on disembarking.

Suddenly Beth and Jon approached through the crowd, looking circumspectly. "I hope you'll come with us today," Beth said.

"Thank you, Beth, I'd be honored."

"Good," Jon said. "We've missed you."

Did he suspect what had taken place between her and Alex? Or did he suspect even worse, that she'd allowed herself to become yet one more victim of "a society out of control" as Beth and Efrem called it?

After a while Beth said, "I'd better try to get ahead of the mob." Today she was in charge of those in the Santa Rosita group who were to tour the ancient Crete city of Knossos.

Efrem was already on the gangway with twenty-five of the group who were to visit Fairhaven on the southern coast, where the apostle Paul's storm-tossed ship had tied up centuries ago.

A numbness overcame Anne Marie. She'd have to forget about Alex and throw herself into the tourist role. After all, Aunt Sylvia had paid thousands of dollars for the trip so that she could do just that.

She realized Jon was waiting for her to speak. She blurted the first thing that came to mind. "I have a special mission here. A teacher friend wants me to buy a piece of Minoan art for her. I think I told you."

He raised his eyebrows. "Important artwork?"

"Not very. She gave me a hundred dollars for it, and it has to fit in my suitcase."

"That makes it easier. But how will you know what she likes?"

"That's easy. Anything with turquoise colors."

"From what I've read about the colors in Minoan art, there will be a little deciding to do."

At the gangway, he stood aside to let her precede him, touching her elbow lightly. "Crete is supposed to be even more interesting than Athens." He looked tentative as his gaze met hers.

"So I've read."

She hoped it was terribly interesting—anything so she could forget. "The cradle of European civilization," she managed to add, recalling the ship's literature. She realized he was trying to keep a conversation going because he was concerned about her.

Down below on the dock, they found their tour bus. She only wanted to sit down, and was relieved that Jon stayed outside to help Beth round up stragglers for Knossos. Finally everyone had produced their tickets and settled on the bus. Jon and Beth climbed aboard.

Beth sat down beside the tour guide, and Jon headed down the aisle toward Anne Marie.

"May I join you?"

He looked so hopeful, she couldn't help saying, "Yes, of course."

But instead of fully welcoming him, she recalled yesterday's trip up to Delphi with Alex, the joy and wonder of being with him...

No! She had to overcome this obsession with Alex. And *obsession* was precisely what it was.

Anne Marie forced her attention back to their tour guide for Crete, a beautiful black-haired girl named Reva. The young woman pointed out the old Venetian fortress with its many arches as well as the other unusual sights as their bus made its way through the city of Heraklion.

"We are much more exotic here than on the Greek mainland," Reva said. "Though we are called *Cretans,* we hope that you will not think of us as *Cretans.*"

Anne Marie's heart was so heavy she could hardly muster a smile, even though the guide's attempt at humor brought chuckles from the others on the bus. She tried to focus on the colorful markets where clothing hung outdoors and the food stalls where fruits and vegetables were displayed.

Outside the city, vineyards and olive groves covered the countryside. But her mind went back to Alex and the sight of him hurrying to the seaplane.

Reva read from Homer, and Anne Marie vaguely recalled having read the same words in a college lit class.

Jon turned toward her. "Do you recall the story from the *Odyssey?*"

She nodded, her mind drifting from the myth of the minotaur and the labyrinth to Alex and his pride in the ancient Greeks.

She forced her attention back to the tour guide's discourse.

Minutes later the bus stopped, and Jon stood back to let her precede him up the bus aisle, the perfect gentleman as always. They stepped out onto the tan rocky soil and made their way to the ancient Crete city, as Reva led them to the vast excavations of Knossos.

Despite her despair, Anne Marie found the ruins amazing. Deep within the labyrinth of Knossos's palace, they followed Reva through the reconstructed throne room with its red walls and alabaster throne. The west wing had been devoted to religious rites, and Anne Marie pondered whether these people had sometimes doubted their faith, too.

Later in the afternoon, their bus returned them to the city of Heraklion. The museum there was primitive, but as she examined delicate pottery and intricate jewelry, Anne Marie slowly began to forget her anguish.

"What strikes me as unusual is the ancients' preoccupation with bulls," Jon said as they passed more murals with death-defying acrobats atop leaping bulls. "I suppose I could easily become an archaeology enthusiast like your friend, Averill."

"I could, too." What Anne Marie wanted to add was that Averill—and Lila—were not her friends.

They toured on, and soon only thirty minutes remained for shopping. Reva pointed out the best shop for artwork in the village, and Jon accompanied Anne Marie to the place. Inside, frescoes painted on plastered wood featured primitive lilies, young men carrying fish, acrobats standing on bulls, ancient galleys being rowed on the sea accompanied by dolphins, and maidens wearing diaphanous attire.

Anne Marie's eyes rested on a cream, russet, and turquoise fresco. Its design showed three maidens in graceful dance, their russet hair streaming behind them. "That's it," she decided. "Turquoise background and 'three maidens all in a row.'"

Jon raised his brow with amusement. "'Three maidens all in a row'? Sounds like a nursery rhyme."

Anne Marie had to smile. "It is. I tend to forget myself at times. An occupational hazzard."

He smiled with her, then turned back to the fresco. "It's rather nice. And it's suitcase-sized." They examined the price in Greek drachmas. Eighty dollars.

"Sheila will love it," Anne Marie said. "She loves dance, too."

Together they bargained the shop owner down to seventy dollars, and before long they were on their way out of the shop, the bubble-wrapped fresco under Jon's arm. It had been a pleasant interlude with Jon. She looked up at him, smiling her appreciation.

He met her gaze and for a moment didn't speak. Then he glanced at his watch. "It's time to get back to the bus."

"How I'd like to come back to absorb all of this for a week or two," Anne Marie wished aloud. *When this heartache over Alex ends.*

"Perhaps you'll come back," Jon said as they headed through the narrow, cobbled streets for their bus.

"I don't think so."

"We never know what God has in mind for us," he said softly. He guided her gently by the elbow over the cobblestones. "I went through a dreadful time in my life, and God has healed my heart of it entirely."

He meant his fiancée's death, she assumed. "How could God heal it?"

"I couldn't handle the pain and gave myself and my problems to him," Jon answered simply.

God had nothing to do with her problems, Anne Marie thought. And now that Alex had walked out of her life, she would never return to Greece nor to its islands. What else could there possibly be for her in this part of the world?

CHAPTER

Nine

When Anne Marie opened her cabin door, she saw the bouquet of pink roses still standing on the dressing table.

"Oh!" She was overcome by anger. How could she have forgotten to dispose of them! Alex had sent them to hurt her—to slap her for rejecting him—and likely he'd chosen *pink* roses to ridicule her. She grabbed the vase, opened the cabin door, and set the roses outside the cabin door so hard that water slopped over.

Beth approached in the corridor. "From Alex?"

"Yes...unfortunately." To her surprise, her voice teetered between anger and tears. "At any rate, pink clashes dreadfully with this gold and purple decor!"

Closing the cabin door behind them, Anne Marie turned to her cabinmate. "How did you know who sent them?"

Beth's green eyes filled with sympathy as she sat down on her bed. "It was a pretty good hint when you threw out the red roses last night."

"I suppose it was."

Beth unlaced her white tennies and pulled them off. "And then there was the minor matter of your being so glum today, not to mention the great drama of Alex's departure by seaplane. It didn't require a rocket scientist to figure something had gone very wrong."

"I assume everyone has figured that out." She turned aside. "It hurts so terribly!"

"I know the feeling all too well," Beth empathized. "I didn't arrive at the ripe old age of thirty-nine without learning some hard lessons of the heart."

"Worst of all, you guessed right on something else, too. He didn't have honorable intentions."

"Unfortunately, I know all too well how that feels, too. The sad fact is that probably most women do nowadays." Beth hesitated. "Nonetheless, I have an inkling that Alex might come back into your life. He strikes me as impetuous and persistent, the type who disappears for a while to lick his wounds, but who isn't accustomed to losing."

"I don't think he'll be back. That was the end of everything between us."

"At least you have someone else who loves you."

"Someone *else* who loves me?" Anne Marie asked. Was Beth going to start in about God loving her? Her Bible had lain open on her bed again this morning...

Beth's green eyes widened. "Haven't you been able to see it? Jon is crazy about you!"

"Jon?"

"Yes, Jon. How could you not notice?"

"I thought he was trying to make amends for his neglect as Aunt Sylvia's attorney. Besides, we're the only two unattached singles in the Santa Rosita group, so we've been paired together." She shook her head. "You must be mistaken."

Her roommate shrugged. "Maybe that's all you feel, but how about Jon? I think he's sorely smitten."

Anne Marie responded bitterly. "He didn't even fly home to

untangle Aunt Sylvia's estate when I needed him. He wasn't even there for her memorial service. She treated him like a son—she loved him so much."

"He must have had a good reason."

"I can't believe it."

How could he have suddenly fallen in love with her on this trip? He'd only seen her the day before they left, then on the plane, and these few days on the ship.

"It's obvious to everyone except you. Even Efrem has remarked about it."

Had she been so enthralled with Alex that she'd noticed nothing else? Certainly the days had been hurtling by so rapidly that she hardly knew which day of the week it was, and she was forever checking the itinerary to know what time the ship would dock next.

"Jon may be experiencing as much hurt as you're feeling now," Beth remarked. "When he's seen you with Alex, he's looked like one of the walking wounded."

"It doesn't seem possible." Besides, she hadn't intentionally hurt Jon or anyone else in her life. "I was so intrigued with him when I was a teenager, but to him I was only the little niece visiting my Aunt Sylvia. He was busy with *real* dates— "

"You've grown up, and I'm sure he realizes it," Beth countered. "It's my guess that he sees you through very different eyes now."

"It's too late, Beth. Just too late."

Beth gave her a soft smile. "I wonder."

As she dressed for dinner, Anne Marie tried to sort out how she felt about Jon. He was charming, intelligent, and an interesting traveling companion. Surely she didn't love him. If anything, she felt he was an old friend in whom she'd been badly disappointed.

Her thoughts returned to Alex, and her heart twisted in agony again. How on earth had Beth overcome her pain the other day when she had been crying with hurt and frustration? How had she returned from the shower with a smile on her face? She'd said that she'd given the problem back to God.

"Beth..." Perhaps she shouldn't ask, but now Beth was waiting and there was no way to evade it. "How do you give a problem to God?"

"Through prayer," Beth answered. "For example, I'd probably say something like 'Heavenly Father, I can't handle this problem myself. Please help me.' And if it's anger at someone, I'd say, 'Give me your love for this person. In the blessed name of Jesus, I pray. Amen.'"

"That's all?"

Beth nodded. "That's all. It sounds pat, but that's how I give problems over to God."

"I don't understand."

"Trust him with it and then move on with life," Beth explained further. "We're not to dwell on life's past problems—only its glad days. We're supposed to wipe the slate of remembrance with love and forget not only our failures but the failures of others. We ask God to help us wipe them from our remembrance because Jesus died for everyone's sins, not just ours."

Beth smiled gently. "In the book of Philippians, the apostle Paul said, 'One thing I do, forgetting those things which are behind, and reaching forth unto those things which are before, I press toward the mark.' That includes ongoing struggles."

"I see," Anne Marie replied, although pressing on sounded easier said than done. "I suppose I should have remembered from Sunday school. In other words, 'Onward!'"

"Only after you entrust God with the problem."

Anne Marie nodded, then quickly changed the subject to what they should wear for dinner. The ship's literature suggested casual attire for the evening. White slacks and a white shirt required no thinking, she decided.

❧

When Efrem picked up Beth for dinner, Jon was nowhere to be seen, and Anne Marie had no inclination to tag along with them. "I'll be there in a while," she said when they urged her to join them.

Yet, when the door closed behind them, she didn't feel like going to the dining room at all. She didn't want to go anywhere. A dark bleakness descended on her.

No! I will not be depressed, she told herself. She had to go to dinner, especially now when she felt like this. She glanced at herself in the cabin mirror and was surprised at how well her reflection looked. The white shirt and slacks were perfect with her tan, and her quickly brushed hair made her look the picture of health. Only her woebegone expression revealed her recent hurt.

An odd thought came to mind: what did she actually have to offer a man like Alex? She'd never considered matters from that angle. She supposed she was fun, at least men told her so. Wholesome fun, not a wild party girl, and usually she was enthusiastic about life. She was an accomplished cook and a good kindergarten teacher; she hoped to be a good wife and mother. And she'd care for Alex as he'd probably never been cared for before! Didn't he see that?

The dinner bells for the seven-thirty seating pealed over the ship's speakers, and she grabbed her cabin key and handbag. She forced a smile at the young woman in the mirror and decided it was a slight improvement, albeit unconvincing.

In the dining room everyone else was already at the table; the only seat left for her was between Efrem and Reynold Williamson.

"Why don't you eat with us tonight?" Nat Nathan looked up at her, a kind expression on his face.

She nodded, remembering that last night she had spent the evening with Alex at the captain's table. The evening had held such promise. "Thank you."

"We can move over so you can sit with Jon," Reynold suggested. "You can't be interested in old fellows like Nat or me, can you?"

"Of course I am. This is fine." She took her seat quickly, trying not to notice Jon, who sat between Beth and Kate Nathan, or the fact that everyone was watching her.

She turned to Efrem. "Did you enjoy your trip to Fairhaven?"

"Yes, indeed, though it's the kind of place that requires a good imagination. There's not much to see of the apostle Paul's stay. Yet I think most of us saw him there in our minds' eyes. It's another piece in his extraordinary life."

Anne Marie scarcely tasted her shrimp cocktail or the prime rib dinner as her thoughts drifted between the dinner conversation and her memory of fleeing from Alex's cabin door. Surely everyone at the table suspected that things had soured between them, perhaps even that she'd been stupid. She skipped dessert and had coffee to be companionable. As she finished her coffee, she found Jon watching her. She forced a smile, then wondered whether it fooled him—or anyone else, for that matter.

When they rose from the table, she wanted to escape as quickly as possible. Best to head for her cabin.

In her haste, she nearly ran down Jon. "I'm sorry!"

"Why the hurry?"

Heat rushed to her face. "Habit, I suppose."

For a while they moved along silently with the dinner crowd, making their way to the dining room doors. He turned to her. "I've been puzzling over how to ask if you'd like to go to the movie with me, and I've decided the best way is to be forthright. Would you like to go to the movie?"

It sounded better than sitting in the cabin reliving last night's heartbreaking scene with Alex. "Thank you. I'd love to." A movie would be a good diversion and wouldn't require conversation.

He grinned encouragingly, and she gave him a small smile in return.

In the crowded elevator going down to the cinema, she stood away from him, but as they stepped into the still-lighted theater, their hands accidentally brushed and he removed his quickly, almost with alarm. Surely Beth was mistaken about Jon being interested in her.

"A nice theater," she remarked as they walked into the cinema auditorium. It held plush, upholstered red chairs, a movie screen on a small stage, and a projection booth in the rear of the room.

"Better than uptown."

The lights dimmed suddenly, and she stopped in the darkness. "I can't see a thing!"

"Here, hold on. One thing about me, I've got great night vision." He took her hand, and she let him lead her until she'd stumbled into a seat.

"I suppose you've been on lots of cruises."

"Nothing like this. Only a few three-day business cruises with a ship full of clients and lawyers from our offices everywhere. For the most part, they are hard work, definitely not vacations."

When they sat down, she moved her hands well away from him. The movie began, and she tried to focus on it, but it was impossible to forget about last night with Alex. Little of the story unfolding on the screen entered her consciousness. Luckily the movie was a mystery and not in the least romantic.

Later, when the movie ended and the lights came on, Jon suggested, "Why don't we get some fresh air on deck."

"Yes, I'd like that." Perhaps it would help her to sleep. She definitely did not need another night full of dreams about Alex.

After taking the elevator up, they admired the window displays outside the ship's boutique, perfume, and jewelry shops. "Look, gold charms for Aunt Sylvia's bracelet. I didn't know you could still buy them, but then I haven't looked, either."

They wandered out to the Promenade Deck and, for a long time, stood looking out at the starlit night and the ship's progress through the inky black sea.

She felt soothed by the rushing sound of the waves. "I could stand here forever."

"God knew what he was doing when he put the waters around us." Jon gave a small laugh. "And man knew what he was doing when he invented cruise ships."

Anne Marie smiled out at the night. "Standing here does make me feel closer to God. I can believe here."

"Can't you believe in God everywhere?"

"I...I do see him in nature. And I do see glimpses of him in life occasionally. But in between, I forget. I just plain forget." Strangely she felt closer to him now and, oddly, closer to Jon, too.

Jon closed his eyes, and she wondered if he was praying for her. If so, it was an endearing sight.

At length he turned to her. "Want to walk around the deck? I notice you skipped dessert, and I thought if we walked long enough, we might hit the yogurt bar down below before turning in."

"Just what I need after eating so much—"

"You didn't eat much dinner either."

She was surprised he'd noticed. "I wasn't very hungry. Okay, let's walk." To change the subject, she said, "Yogurt seems so

American, it's hard to figure such a food on a Greek ship."

"As I recall, yogurt had its beginning in the Balkan countries—I think Bulgaria."

"You do know all kinds of interesting tidbits."

His eyes met hers. "That I do. They clutter up the brain but make life more interesting."

She managed a smile.

They walked twenty vigorous turns around the deck before they allowed themselves to visit the yogurt bar. Decorated like an ice cream parlor, it was tucked into an aft corner of the Promenade Deck, and offered vanilla, chocolate, strawberry, and lemon yogurt—and a vast variety of toppings.

"Chocolate," Anne Marie told the young man behind the bar. "Umm...for toppings, I think I'll have hot fudge, nuts, and some sprinkles." She turned ruefully to Jon. "We'll have to make twenty more turns around the deck."

"I'm game." He ordered the same. "I'm a chocoholic myself. Amazingly, I haven't had hot fudge in years."

They carried their desserts to a soda fountain table, settled into the curved wire chairs, and dug in.

As they sat eating, it occurred to Anne Marie that this should have happened years ago, perhaps after the memorable day on the lake when Jon had braided her hair.

Later, when they walked outside to the back of the deck, they looked out at the night again.

"I guess I couldn't stay out here all night after all," she said. "I'm beginning to realize how tired I am."

"No wonder. You've had an exhausting day."

She wondered if he was referring in part to Alex's dramatic departure by seaplane. "Yes, we did walk a lot in Crete— "

Jon's arm moved around her, turning her to him.

"Jon!" she began to protest.

In the moonlight, the angular planes of his face made him

look even more appealing. “Please, Anne Marie, give me a chance. I know you must think I don’t deserve it...”

She saw a boyish hopefulness in his eyes that touched her heart. She turned her face up to his.

His lips touched hers softly, almost reverently. She slipped her hands around his neck, and her fingers moved through his hair just as she’d dreamed those summers when she was a girl.

Suddenly, reason reasserted itself, and she stepped back. “No more...”

“You’re right,” he agreed firmly.

What was wrong with her? Last night she’d run from Alex’s advances and now she was returning Jon’s kiss. What sort of a woman was she?

Jon looked at the night sky. “I can’t say I’m sorry, but it was unplanned, no matter what you might think. Unplanned but wonderful.”

She decided not to encourage him. “I think it’s time for me to turn in.”

Outside her cabin door she wondered if he might try to kiss her again, but he only looked at her with concern. She quickly unlocked the cabin door and rushed in. “Good night, Jon. I can’t imagine what you must think of me.”

“I think you’re a very lovely young woman.” He stopped, as if he wanted to say something else, then only added, “Good night, Anne Marie.”

She closed the door and leaned weakly against it. How could she have gotten into such a situation? It had been another matter when she’d been a teenager, but now?

Once in bed, she lay awake for a long while. Her mind wandered to memories of Alex, and she relived her childhood scenes with him—and last night’s flight from his cabin door. Her thoughts moved on to Jon and their kiss. Gentle, but with a hint of subdued passion. Despite her anger at him, she had to admit he was a gentleman.

Lying in bed exhausted, she recalled snatches of a song Aunt Sylvia used to sing, "One day at a time…one day at a time…" She tried to remember the rest, but the words floated away until at last she slept.

Before dawn she felt the ship slowing as it sailed through the Dardanelles and into the Sea of Marmara. She heard Beth get up but was too tired to fully awaken.

When Anne Marie arrived on the Promenade Deck at nine o'clock for a continental breakfast, the sunshine was so dazzling and the Sea of Marmara so blue that it appeared they had sailed beyond reality.

At a table near the ship's polished railing, she ate pineapple and melon chunks, then an apple muffin with her coffee. Finished, she took the book she'd purchased at the ship's gift shop to the shaded side of the deck. She wore a white terry cover-up over her turquoise bathing suit. She took off the wrap before laying down on a lounge in the sun.

She read in snatches, but the song that had eased her into sleep haunted her: "One day at a time…one day at a time…" She tried not to think about Alex, tried not to hear him in every Greek accent aboard ship, tried not to see him in every man with dark hair and eyes.

When lunch was announced, she pulled on her beach cover-up and joined Beth and Efrem, who'd been sunning among other members of their group on the aft deck. A sumptuous fare had been set out on the buffet tables: shrimp, crab, tuna, and chicken salads; fruit; hot vegetables and entrees; and of course, a heavily laden dessert table.

Eating at a shaded starboard side table with Beth and Efrem, she glimpsed Jon coming toward them with his lunch tray.

"May I join you?" He acted as if nothing of significance had happened between them last night.

"Of course," Efrem answered heartily.

Jon looked at Anne Marie.

"Certainly. Here, let me take my beach bag from the chair."

He settled down beside her at the white wooden table, appearing quite at ease. He'd just been on a tour of the engine room he explained, and began to tell about it.

For a curious moment Anne Marie saw the four of them—Jon and her, Beth and Efrem—as an abstract painting, as if they had been thickly brushed with oils in her mind. There were the bright colors of their holiday clothing, their white smiles against their tans as they squinted against the sun and its reflection on the sea. It was as if the four of them, complicated lives and all, had been painted in time.

At length, she realized Jon was watching her.

"How are you, Anne Marie? Rested?"

She pushed aside a chunk of chicken and speared a black olive. "Yes," she replied. "I spent the morning reading in the shade."

He dug in his pants pocket and pulled out a small box. "I have a little present for you."

"But you shouldn't—"

"I wanted to," he replied with a smile. "Open it."

Slowly overcoming her reluctance, she accepted the box, then took off the thin gold cord around it. As she opened the gift, she said, "Oh, Jon..."

On a bed of white cotton lay two gleaming charms: one of the Parthenon, the other of a Cretan acrobat on a bull's back.

"Charms of places you've visited for your—and Aunt Sylvia's—bracelet," he said. "It's a good way to remember, and I noticed there are still a few places on the chain for more."

"They're lovely, but I can't accept such an expensive gift."

"Of course you can accept a gift from an old friend."

"They're beautiful," Beth said as she and Efrem admired the tiny charms.

"*Charming* if I do say so," Efrem teased, causing them all to chuckle.

Anne Marie met Jon's eyes and found herself unable to refuse.

"For the rest of your life when you wear the bracelet, you can remember Athens and Crete," Jon said.

And you, Jon, something inside her said, unbidden.

She recalled the day spent in Athens with Alex—and the day with Jon in Crete. What mixed emotions and memories! And now there were gold charms to remember it all by.

Jon added, "It seemed a much better idea than postcards. Besides, the charms are so beautifully crafted I had to buy them for someone. I don't suppose Efrem would let me give them to Beth."

Beth laughed. "Not that you've tried to!"

"And not that I could afford them," Efrem said.

"Just consider them a gift from an old friend," Jon repeated. "After all, we've known each other for years now. Why, I even remember your braces."

"Never mind about them!"

They all laughed.

"Thank you, Jon," she said. "I'll treasure the charms."

She wondered if he'd given them to her because of last night's kiss. Or because of guilt at not being at Aunt Sylvia's memorial service.

"Istanbul in the distance!" Efrem announced. "You can just barely make it out."

They turned to the sunstruck whiteness of the distant city beyond the sea, and passengers rushed to the railings to marvel at the scene.

Beth squinted into the sunlight. "Istanbul is supposed to be the most beautiful city in the world when coming in by sea."

"It is, as far as I've seen." Efrem shaded his eyes, gazing at the still-distant city.

Anne Marie marveled, "It surely is for me."

By the time the ship approached the Golden Horn, they'd not only finished lunch, but also rushed to their cabins to use the facilities and gather up their cameras.

Passengers stood at the railings as they approached the exotic city. The bustling waterway held yachts, ocean liners, freighters, tankers, and old ferry boats belching black smoke.

An announcement crackled over the ship's loudspeaker, heightening the excitement. "Because so many ships are in port, the *Golden Isle* will have to drop anchor. Our tender boats will ferry passengers ashore."

Slowly, the *Golden Isle* maneuvered into the fray, and young Turks waved from row boats darting about them as the ship followed a pilot boat to their designated anchorage.

Once there, the anchor chain clanged off the deck and into the sea. They stopped before Istanbul's skyline of modern skyscrapers interspersed with mosques, minarets, and centuries-old buildings.

Beth's voice was soft with awe as she stood watching from the railing. "Turkey!"

Anne Marie stood beside Beth, a breeze lifting wisps of her hair. "Just the idea of it conjures up ghostly sultans and veiled women in harems."

Soon they made their way to the Mediterranean Deck for disembarking, and Anne Marie thought most of the passengers felt as excited as she. The ship's tender boats were lowered one by one, and passengers began to climb down a metal gangway to the small tender boats waiting far below in the water.

"I don't want to look!" Anne Marie protested when it was her turn to climb down.

Jon moved forward to stand near her. "I'll go first. Don't worry, I'll catch you if you fall."

"Thanks a lot!"

She felt certain, however, that he would catch her, if necessary. Behind her, Beth and Efrem made their way down. At long last, a crewman helped her board the small tender boat, and she followed Jon to the empty seats.

"It wasn't as bad as I thought it would be," she sighed as they sat down. She often had a way of worrying about matters that turned out to be simple in the end. It suddenly occurred to her that the same might be true with Christianity.

A young Turk in a nearby rowboat hawked his wares at her in broken English. "Worry beads, lady? Post cards?" He nodded at Jon. "A jeweled dagger to kill the husband?"

Her *husband!*

She laughed and glanced at an equally amused Jon as other passengers climbed aboard. Finally, the tender boat roared off for the dock.

When they disembarked from the tender onto the dock, smiling bus drivers waited by the tour buses, and everyone piled in excitedly, anticipating adventure. It seemed only moments later that their bus was edging into the wild traffic.

Their bus horn blared outrageously, and everyone burst into laughter, then applause. Anne Marie couldn't help but compare everyone on the bus, herself included, to a class of delighted kindergarten children out on a marvelously exciting field trip.

Efrem pointed out the famous bridge linking Europe with Asia, gleaming in the distance. Through the open bus windows, *ezan*, the Arabic call to prayer, wailed eerily from a nearby minaret.

"It's a dream," Anne Marie said. "This is a dream."

"We're here," Jon answered from beside her, although judging by his voice, he sounded excited, too.

Outside on the streets, dark-haired men milled about,

reminding her of Alex, though she couldn't imagine him in Turkey. Just days ago he'd proclaimed, "Greeks are Greeks, and Turks are Turks, and never shall the twain meet!"

The bus stopped to let their group off in an antiquated section of the city, and Anne Marie followed the group into a richly-appointed Greek Orthodox church. A black robed priest wearing a tall black miter on his head welcomed each of them with the help of a translator. There seemed a special poignancy to the moment while Anne Marie shook hands with him. Despite their differences in language, his eyes spoke of joyous love.

Later, as she left the church and stepped out into the centuries-old street, the aroma of baking bread filled the air, and the group members laughed to find themselves already hungry. Jon and the elderly Nathans rushed to the nearby bakery and emerged minutes later with bags full of sesame seed rolls that gave off a mouth-watering fragrance.

On the bus, Anne Marie noticed again that everyone assumed she and Jon would sit together. In any event, no one sat down in the empty seat beside her. And when Jon passed along the aisle offering the sesame seed rolls to everyone, she heard an elderly man inquire, "Where did your wife go?"

"We're friends, only friends," he explained quietly.

"You should be friends if you're married," the man said as if he hadn't heard well.

"I think so, too," Jon replied with amusement.

He turned to Anne Marie, but she pretended to be preoccupied with the scene outside her window.

He settled beside her, offering her a fragrant roll. "They're ambrosial." He sat back as if nothing disconcerting had been mentioned.

She bit into the roll uneasily, thinking that Jon must feel as embarrassed as she. Twice within hours they had been mistaken for a married couple. Actually, it was rather amusing.

"It's delicious," she said, munching on the roll happily.

Later, at the sprawling Grand Bazaar, vendors hawked antiques, carpets, copperware, silver, gold, leather coats, and jeweled harem slippers.

"Come here, lady, nice jewelry!" they shouted at Anne Marie from their colorful stalls. "Nice copper, lady!" "Turkish rugs, gold jewelry!" "Embroideries, brocades—very cheap, double price!"

She and Jon concealed their amusement over the vendor's contorted English and moved on through the maze of five thousand shops. Despite their determination not to lose their way, they became wildly confused in the tangle of shops and streets. When they finally found their way to the bus, they laughed with heartfelt relief.

In the evening, the bus took them to a seaside restaurant on the Bosporus Strait, where they dined on a delectable seafood dinner and watched the bustling seagoing traffic through the windows. With such a congenial crowd, Anne Marie thought of Alex less and less, and Jon was an attentive escort, his hand solicitously at her elbow whenever needed.

During the night, the *Golden Isle* had moved to Istanbul's main dock, and in the morning there was no need to disembark by tender. Anne Marie could hardly take in all the sights as they toured Byzantine churches and ruins, fortresses, museums, magnificent mosques, and then Topkapi Palace.

Inside the palace, she and Jon followed their guide through some of the four-hundred gilded and gaudily tiled harem rooms. Tattered couches brought to mind reclining sultans who watched the dancing girls, and there were royal marble baths and carved, inlaid bedchambers.

How peculiar to view all of this, Anne Marie thought. She

noticed, too, that the young woman who guided them seemed embarrassed about Turkey's harem days.

Later, the group marveled at the treasures: doorknob-sized diamonds, eye-popping emeralds, magnificent jeweled daggers and swords, precious china and glassware—all of exquisite quality. She wondered if Alex would ever see these amazing treasures. Probably not. Why had the rancor between Greeks and Turks lasted so many centuries? Why couldn't they forgive and forget? On the other hand, why couldn't she forgive and forget, either?

When the *Golden Isle* sailed, she and Jon stood at the railing to watch Istanbul disappear in the distance. "Magnificent, isn't it?"

"Yes, and different from anywhere I've ever been or anywhere I'll probably ever go again."

"You never know." His tone was uneasy.

She glanced at him as he looked out at the city over the Sea of Marmara. Whatever relationship had existed before between them had subtly changed while they were ashore. Despite their moonlit kiss, a tenuousness had grown between them, an atmosphere of wait and see, and she knew it wasn't merely her restraint because of Alex. Jon was holding back, too.

On Sunday morning, soft sunshine glistened on the port town of Kusadasi, Turkey, as Anne Marie hurried down the gangway of the *Golden Isle*. When she stood for a moment on the dock with Jon, she looked around for birds. "I thought 'Kusadasi' meant 'island of the birds,'" she said, disappointed. "There's nothing but sea gulls."

Jon chuckled as the gray and white gulls wheeled over the blue water near the dock. "And it's not actually an island either."

The only visible island lay just across the water. Dominating the small piece of land was a picturesque Ottoman Empire fortress whose centuries-old walls displayed a bright red banner that proclaimed *Restaurant.*

"Tourism transforms the world," Jon remarked.

In high spirits, they started for the line of tour buses waiting beyond the dock. Since they'd been among the first passengers off the ship, they had time to look around.

The morning air sparkled about the small port town, whose current reason for existence seemed to be as a shopping stop for the hordes of tourists enroute to Ephesus. Everyone in the Santa Rosita group was especially thrilled at the prospect of visiting the city. The tour guide had already told them that Ephesus was the ancient city where both the apostles Paul and John had preached in the first century and where the Virgin Mary had supposedly lived out her latter years.

"Postcards, lady?" Turkish vendors called to Anne Marie. "Ephesus book?"

She shook her head vehemently, but they dashed after her through the crowd of passengers disembarking from the four cruise ships at the dock.

"Leather wallets! Handbags!" The shouts followed her in English, French, and German. Small boys hawked copper and tin bells, blue evil-eye necklaces, and "silver necklace for one dollar." Jon stopped to buy a colorful guide book about Ephesus from a dark-haired boy, and instantly they were surrounded by others expecting sales.

"Are you sure you don't want harem slippers?" Jon teased Anne Marie as the boys thrust the ornate slippers at her.

She laughed. "I'm positive about that."

Jon caught her arm to help her through the swarming vendors who lined the way to the tour buses.

They sat near the front of the tour bus, but it was some time before the bus pulled away. Before long, they rode beyond Kusadasi's cobbled tourist area and climbed the hillsides to the ruins of Ephesus.

Their young guide introduced herself from the front of the bus as they bounced through the countryside. Beside her, the bus driver blasted the horn at a herd of goats on the road, then at sheep and cattle, while everyone laughed.

As they rode along, Anne Marie became uncomfortably aware of Jon's nearness. Glancing at him in profile, she noticed a lock of his hair hung slightly across his high forehead; she felt oddly tempted to brush it back into place. Her eyes wandered over his high cheekbones and angular chin, then to his lips. It was a strong face, different in profile than when he looked at her with those unsettling blue eyes.

"Something wrong?" He turned toward her and his eyes met hers.

"No...no...nothing."

She was grateful that their attention was diverted by camels along the roadside, then a stork on the rooftop of one of the small Turkish rock houses.

"Turkey is an exciting country for Christians." The guide looked out over the group. "The seven cities mentioned in the Book of Revelation are here: Ephesus, Smyrna, Pergamos, Thyatira, Sardis, Philadelphia, and Laodicea."

Before long, she pointed out a sign: *To Izmir.*

"Once known as Smyrna," Jon said. "Famous for figs."

"Ah, a student of history." The guide's eyes reflected respect.

As they glanced out, Anne Marie decided that she liked Jon's interest in history, geography, and religion—his intellect.

Then there was Alex. Unfortunately, "out of sight, out of mind," definitely did not apply to him. What foolishness love was between men and women, she told herself, and decided to focus instead on ancient history.

The guide said, "In the distance you see the ruins of the sixth-century basilica where St. John was buried. According to some scholars, the Virgin Mary lies buried there, too. We are told that Jesus gave his mother into the care of John."

When they climbed off the bus at the entrance to Ephesus, Anne Marie felt as if she'd stepped back through time to the first century.

The guide stood on a small incline and looked down at the group. "Here, one civilization is built atop another. Antony and Cleopatra dallied here. The Temple of Artemis was one of the seven wonders of the ancient world. When Alexander the Great discovered the temple in ruins, he offered to rebuild it—as long as it bore his name. His offer was respectfully refused on the grounds that it would not be fitting for one god to make a dedication to another."

Jon chuckled with the others. "Real diplomacy."

Anne Marie smiled, then turned her camera on the archaeological site. "We'll never capture all of this," she sighed. "There's no way to do it justice."

"We'll give it a try." Jon searched through his camera case for his wide angle lens. "Wish I'd bought a video camera."

As she snapped pictures, she noticed Averill Thornton surveying the ruins alone. Where was Lila? She hadn't seen the woman since Alex left.

Later, they made their way through the ruins of the gymnasium, the town hall and fountains, levels of pillars and statues, baths, temples, and the stadium not far from what had once been the world-famous seaport.

Finally, they assembled at the end of a marble avenue away from the crowds of tourists.

As they quieted, Efrem began to speak. "Today we walked where the apostles Paul and John and perhaps the mother of Jesus walked. When Paul arrived in Ephesus, he asked the disciples he found there, 'Did you receive the Holy Spirit when you believed?'

"'What is the Holy Spirit?' they asked.

"'Then what kind of a baptism did you receive?' Paul asked. They replied, 'The baptism of John.'"

Efrem paused. "Paul told these disciples that John's baptism was for those who turned from their sins, and that those receiving his baptism must then go on to believe in Jesus, who John the Baptist said would come later."

Efrem stopped again for emphasis. "When they heard that, they were baptized in the name of the Lord Jesus, and the Holy Spirit came on them."

Anne Marie frowned, wondering what it meant—*the Holy Spirit came on them.*

"After that," Efrem continued, "Paul went to the synagogue and for three months preached each Sabbath, persuading many to believe in Jesus. Some rejected his message and spoke against Christ, so Paul left, taking his disciples with him."

Efrem smiled. "Paul was indefatigable. His preaching went on for the next two years, so that everyone in this province—Jews and Greeks—heard the Lord's message. God was performing unusual miracles of healing through Paul, too. Even handkerchiefs or parts of clothing he'd used were taken to the sick and they were healed."

Healed? Surely these people from Santa Rosita didn't believe in that! Anne Marie glanced at the crowd, but they listened to Efrem in rapt attention.

"Then the trouble started." Efrem's voice dropped. "It began with a silversmith who made shrines of the Greek goddess Diana. Calling a meeting, he said, 'This Paul tells people that handmade gods aren't gods at all. Our sales are falling all over the province!'"

Anne Marie grimaced at Jon, whose expression reflected

hers. As usual, people had put themselves first.

Efrem continued, "The crowd became furious and shouted, 'Great is Diana of Ephesus!' The uproar spread over the city. The mob rushed to the amphitheater, grabbing Paul's companions. Paul wanted to speak to the crowd, but his disciples and Roman friends with authority begged him not to speak. Finally, a city official calmed everyone and dispersed them to avoid trouble with Rome over the day's riot."

"Business and politics as usual," Jon remarked.

Anne Marie nodded.

"When the riot was over," Efrem said, "Paul called for his disciples and, after encouraging them, said farewell. He left for Greece and preached all the way. The next time Paul was near Ephesus, he asked that the elders of the church come down to his boat to avoid entering the city again."

Opening her eyes, Anne Marie glanced out to where the seaport had stood, visualizing how it must have been.

Efrem went on. "When they arrived, Paul told them again. 'I have the same message for Jews and Gentiles alike—turn from sin to God, through faith in our Lord Jesus Christ.'

"And that," Efrem concluded, "is our message from Paul today. We must turn from sin to God through faith in our Lord Jesus Christ."

After a while, the group moved on through the ancient ruins, and Anne Marie saw Jon waiting for her to join him. She wondered again what Aunt Sylvia had meant about his return to their faith.

Did it mean that the Holy Spirit had actually manifested itself upon him in a discernible way?

Had he experienced something supernatural?

Suddenly she felt uneasy about it. What had she gotten herself into on this trip? And they had yet to reach Israel!

CHAPTER

Ten

The *Golden Isle* sailed across the sparkling blue Mediterranean as Anne Marie, Jon, Beth, and Efrem sat at a Promenade Deck table eating lunch. It seemed impossible that only hours ago they had walked through centuries-old ruins at Ephesus.

Jon glanced out at the calm sea. "We haven't had a hint of the infamous Mediterranean storms yet."

"Don't even mention it!" Efrem laughed. "The apostle Paul endured enough storms and shipwrecks for all of us! It's enough to imagine it."

"Imagination is such an interesting faculty," Anne Marie remarked. At their curious glances, she tried to explain. "Seeing the ruins and giving my imagination free rein, I could see the past taking place at stops like Corinth and Ephesus. When I studied history at school, historic sites didn't take on much reality."

Efrem raised his brows. "Not everyone can see beyond the surface of even the most intriguing archaeological sites. Some never see beyond the old stones. Let's take a poll here." He asked Jon, "Did you visualize the ancients at the sites?"

"To a limited extent," Jon answered agreeably. "At Ephesus, for example, I could nearly see Paul telling the people about Christ in the amphitheater."

Strange, she'd stood beside him without in the least suspecting what was going on in his mind, Anne Marie thought.

Efrem inquired of her, "What specifically did you visualize?"

"I could see Paul speaking to the church elders out in his ship when he returned," she told them. "It's rather like a painting in my head except the people move, first down to the ship, waving at Paul, delighted to see him again. They embrace him..."

She stopped, turning to Beth. "Am I the only one? Couldn't you imagine it?"

"A little," Beth answered. "When I saw the medical symbol on the bas-relief there, I began to imagine the sick and the crippled coming to Paul for healing."

"The one-time nurse among us speaks." Jon smiled at Beth. "But do you believe in healing?"

She nodded. "I believe all healing is from God, that he planned it. But if you mean instantaneous healing, even some of the newer nursing textbooks discuss the laying on of hands. It's become an up-to-date concept again."

"You mean instantaneous healing actually happens?" Anne Marie asked with more than a grain of disbelief.

Beth nodded. "It can."

"And you, Efrem?" Jon asked. "What did you see among the ancients at Ephesus?"

Efrem pressed his lips together. "I saw the doubts and unbelief in the people's eyes when Paul preached, and his perseverance."

"Like you, Efrem," Beth said. "You persevere."

"Praise God for that," Efrem responded. "I don't always want to, though."

They grew silent, and it occurred to Anne Marie that it must sadden Efrem to see people with doubts like hers.

As they rose from the table, Efrem said, "It'll be interesting to hear what each of us visualizes at Patmos." He explained to Anne Marie, "It's where the apostle John received the Book of Revelation."

It would certainly be interesting, Anne Marie thought. She only knew that the Book of Revelation was the last book of the Bible and full of prophecies; a blessing was promised for those who read it.

Later, Efrem presented a port-of-call talk for the Santa Rosita group. "At Patmos, Christ swept back the curtain of eternity and gave John a glimpse of what heaven was like," he told them. "John sat in the grotto hearing the voice of God. Through his writings, we get a first hand account of his unforgettable experience."

Anne Marie glanced at Jon, who listened intently. Did he believe it?

"Revelation is the doctrine of God's making himself and relevant truths known to men," Efrem continued. "There are two kinds of revelations: general and specific. General revelations are communicated through nature, conscience, and history. Special revelations are given to particular people at particular times—although they may be intended for others as well—and come chiefly through the Bible and Jesus Christ."

After the talk, Anne Marie hurried to her cabin to tidy up before the stop at Patmos, all the while pondering Efrem's explanation. True, she saw God revealed in nature—in the wonders of the sky and of the earth, in the beauty of flowers, birds, butterflies...

She supposed she'd heard his still voice at times in her conscience, as well. Why else had she fled from Alex that night by his cabin when it might have taken less strength of character to stay with him?

But in history? What she saw now in the archaeological sites? It added up to more evidence.

And special revelation? Nothing of that sort had ever been revealed to her, but then she didn't read the Bible, or attend church. What's more, she felt decidedly suspicious of people who called Jesus their friend.

Did Efrem mean that special revelations still came to people today?

Shortly after three o'clock, the distant hills of Patmos rose above the brilliant sea. When Anne Marie joined the passengers lining up for the gangway, the *Golden Isle* was already maneuvering into the small island's magnificent deep bay. It was surely one of the most awesome natural sights of the trip. And crowning the mountain, stood the fortress walls that surrounded the Monastery of St. John.

Once down the gangway, Anne Marie looked again around the dock and the quaint village square for the Santa Rosita group. Her heart warmed to see Jon waiting for her near the tour buses, and there were the Nathans and the Williamsons with Beth and Efrem. Their group was becoming a family. What a shame it would be to take this trip alone!

Beth checked off names from her clipboard list as Anne Marie and Jon climbed on the bus.

"That's everybody," Beth said.

"Let's go!" Efrem told the bus driver.

Within minutes, the bus was winding up a steep hillside road with terrifying hairpin turns. Sitting with Jon, Anne Marie was torn between not looking out at their impending destruction or missing the glorious panorama of hills, white-washed villages, and brilliant blue sea. "I can't bear to look out anymore!" she protested at one particularly precarious turn.

"Why worry?" Kate Nathan turned to look back at Anne Marie from the seat in front of them. "The worst that can happen is that we'd go to glory!" She sounded absolutely calm about it; if anything, she seemed to relish the idea of her spirit blithely flying away.

Anne Marie swallowed uneasily. It was the kind of thing her aunt might have said, but as far as Anne Marie Gardene was concerned, it was best not to dwell on death.

"Your face is white!" Jon smiled at her. "Here, hold onto me."

She let him tuck her hand under his muscular arm and closed her eyes as the bus approached the next hairpin turn. It was comforting to hold onto him, and when she opened her eyes, he gave her another smile of assurance.

At the top of the mountain, the bus let off the passengers near the white-washed monastery. Above them stood gray, fortresslike rock walls, terraced roofs, and banks of white bell towers. Turning again to the sea, it seemed impossible to believe that the beautiful island had once been a penal colony where political prisoners had been condemned to hard labor. The apostle John—then the bishop of Ephesus—had been exiled here for preaching about Jesus.

"A glorious prison," Jon remarked.

The two of them followed the others into the eleventh-century monastery, where towering white-washed walls and arches rose in stark contrast to the brilliant blue sky overhead. The incredible beauty of the setting stunned everyone into reverent silence.

After a long while, Anne Marie murmured to Jon, "I'm never going to want to quit traveling."

"It does become addictive," he replied.

They wandered slowly through the white monastery rooms open to tourists, awed by the simple beauty. In the treasury, however, there were Byzantine jewels and embroidery, carved screens, a priceless icon, and a silver shrine.

In the library, a young, black-robed monk explained, "This is the *Codex Purpureus,* our finest treasure—a fragment of the Gospel of St. Mark, handwritten on purple vellum in the sixth century." His fellow monks moved slowly among the glass-encased manuscripts as if the bustle of the world was entirely foreign to them.

Anne Marie and Jon stepped outside on an upper level to take pictures, aiming their cameras at the white-washed terraces and bell towers. Nearby, a white-bearded monk smiled so beatifically that she remembered from childhood, "Except ye be as little children, ye shall not enter into the kingdom of heaven."

Surely this elderly man was one of them. "You can see the love in his eyes," she said to Jon.

"Yes, you can see quite a lot in people's eyes. I suppose that's why they're often called the 'windows of the soul.'"

What did he see in her eyes? she wondered. What did others see? There was also something in the Bible about "putting away childish things."

All too soon, it was time to leave.

Slowly, the bus followed the precipitous curves down the mountainside, stopping halfway to drop the passengers off near the Church of the Apocalypse.

As they walked to the church, Jon read from the guidebook: "The voice of God spoke to St. John through a threefold crack in the rock, and St. John—to whom alone it was audible—dictated to his disciple, Prochorus."

Inside, they found a young monk studying by the grotto. He pointed to three cracks in the ceiling. "Through them God spoke to John: 'I am the Alpha and the Omega, the First and the Last. Write down everything you see.'"

Anne Marie's heart quickened.

The monk indicated a place on the floor. "And here the good saint rested his head." He pointed at a slope in the rock wall Prochorus used as his desk while John dictated, and a grip by which John raised himself from his knees after long hours of prayer.

Candlelight flickered through the enshrined grotto, and Anne Marie felt a pure reverence. If only she could hear God, if only she could be closer and never doubt. She yearned for assurance. *I want to believe,* something in her wished, but her longing went unfulfilled.

After a time Jon whispered, "The bus is waiting."

She hurried out with him into the blinding sunshine, jolted into the present. She'd felt so far away, far beyond time and reality.

On the bus she looked out over the island's idyllic panorama, and the precarious drops from the roadside didn't bother her quite as much. It was such a majestic place, this tiny island of Patmos.

Later, Jon stood companionably with her at the railing as the *Golden Isle* sailed away. She was serene as the white houses in the villages and the white crown of the monastery grew smaller and smaller. Before long, she saw only a hilly island with patches of green trees in the blue sea.

Her serenity lingered as she walked to her cabin to change for the evening's casual dinner. For the first time in days, she felt entirely peaceful. As she opened the cabin door, she saw an envelope on the floor. It was addressed, *Ms. Anne Marie Gardene.*

Hands suddenly trembling, Anne Marie picked up the envelope and tore it open.

Truly sorry for the misunderstanding, the faxed message said. *Must see you. Will be waiting at the dock in Rhodes tonight. Alex.*

She reread the words.

It couldn't have been easy for Alex to send such a message with Andropoulos employees reading it on the ship. She recalled Beth's prediction about Alex returning, about him being impetuous but persistent.

Minutes later when Beth stopped by the cabin, Anne Marie still held the fax in her hand. "I can't go to dinner. I can't eat—"

"Do you have a fever?" Beth asked, reaching a hand to Anne Marie's forehead.

She stepped back quickly. "Alex is meeting me in Rhodes tonight. I just received a fax."

Beth dropped her hand, her green eyes widening. "But what—" She stopped, although Anne Marie felt certain her cabinmate was going to ask about Jon.

"Alex apologized for our...misunderstanding."

"I can't think what to say," Beth began. "Only that if you're pleased, then I'm delighted for you."

Anne Marie hugged her cabinmate. "Oh, Beth, I'm so happy. And I'm so happy to have you for a friend!"

Beth might consider Jon far more suitable, but if so, she had the good sense to keep it to herself.

"You'll tell Jon and Efrem?"

"If you want me to, I will," Beth answered.

It was nearly ten in the evening when the *Golden Isle* maneuvered through to the dimly lit dock at the Greek island of Rhodes. The medieval city walls were bright with light, however, throwing the towers and battlements into relief against the black night sky. It appeared that they'd sailed into the midst of a Crusader's setting.

Anne Marie stood at the railing, peering down at the dock for Alex, but it was too dark to recognize him among the small figures waiting below. She considered his intentions. Did he suppose they could begin all over again because he'd apologized?

And then there was Jon.

It wasn't as if she were betraying him. They'd shared no promises. For several long moments she stared out toward Rhodes, thinking hard.

"There you are!" Beth exclaimed. "Aren't you getting off the ship?"

Jon and Efrem stood on deck with Beth, the lighted medieval castle behind them.

Anne Marie shook her head at herself. "I can't imagine what I was thinking. I was a million miles away."

She followed Beth to the disembarkation line. The atmosphere was tense, and Anne Marie could only assume that her cabinmate had broken the news of Alex's return.

As they waited, Jon read from the Rhodes guidebook. "Things to do in the evening: gamble in the casino, visit the tavernas, shop in old town."

"Doesn't leave too many choices for a preacher, does it?" Beth teased Efrem.

"Oh, I don't know about that," he laughed. "Usually I have more fun than others, just being with people."

Beth smiled fondly at him. "People have even more fun being with you!"

Anne Marie glanced uneasily at Jon.

His eyes met hers for a moment, and she quickly looked away. What could she say to him? He ought to understand her situation. Finally, they arrived at the gangway. Hurrying down, she squinted out onto the dimly lit dock for Alex. There! Was that Alex?

When she stepped off the gangway, he hurried toward her, Lila and Averill Thornton in tow.

"Anne Marie!" Alex called out, opening his arms wide

She stopped well in front of him, knowing that Jon and the others were behind her. She was not going to run into Alex's arms in front of them.

"How are you, Alex?" she asked coolly.

He caught her by the shoulders, taken by surprise, then quickly beamed at Lila and Averill. "It appears I am in trouble."

Anne Marie saw Jon, Beth, and Efrem moving on toward the city with the stream of passengers and felt relieved.

"Didn't you receive my fax?" Alex asked. "If you have it, you know what I said."

"Yes," she answered, aware of the Thorntons listening to them. Perhaps if he were less public about this, she would feel more forgiving.

Alex led her away.

"Do you forgive me?" he asked softly, looking as repentant as one of her kindergarten boys caught in mischief. "I should have known you were not like so many other women."

She sighed, smiling up at him. "How can I not forgive you when you put it that way?"

He embraced her exuberantly, kissing her hair as she ducked her head. "Wonderful! Wonderful!" he exclaimed. "Now let's get a taxi. Tonight we shall surely break the casino!"

She pulled away from him. "The casino?"

"You don't want to go with us?"

"I...It's just that I'd rather see Rhodes. Tomorrow we'll barely have time to see Lindos, and the ship sails at noon—"

"Then tonight you shall see Rhodes," Alex announced. "Anything to make you happy. Anything."

He turned to the Thorntons. "Anne Marie and I will make a tour of the city. Go on to the casino. Let me get you a taxi."

Anne Marie's heart sang. He did care. He did.

He seemed in wonderful spirits as he flagged a taxi for the Thorntons, then held its back door open for them.

Lila looked up at him as she slipped into the seat with a flash of slim legs. "I'll see you later," she said meaningfully.

Anne Marie told herself firmly that the woman was merely trying to make trouble. That first night Alex had remarked about Lila liking to "stir the pot." That's all that it was. It occurred to her that she hadn't even seen Lila since Alex had left that dismal morning in Crete. Averill had been alone at the ruins in Ephesus.

"Don't worry about it, Alex," Averill said, climbing into the cab behind Lila. "You know we can manage very well."

"Just so you don't break the bank entirely," Alex replied with a laugh.

As the taxi pulled away, he slipped his arm around Anne Marie's shoulders.

"If you'd rather go to the casino, I'll catch up with my friends," she offered.

He pulled her close. "I'd rather be with you. Much rather."

"And play tour guide again?"

"Even to play tour guide again," he responded, "especially if I can convince you to begin with a kiss."

She was surprised to find herself resisting.

"You don't want to?" he asked.

"I don't know, Alex. Can't we take this opportunity to learn more about each other?"

He smiled slowly at her in the dim light. "So that's it. I'm moving too fast for you, aren't I?"

"You make me...confused."

He caught her hand and brought it to his lips, kissing her fingertips. "I'm sorry. I'm truly sorry."

"I am too. I don't know what I expected."

"Nor I," he said. "My work has been a trial to me and to everyone in my vicinity lately. My family says I've become a bear, that I need a rest. That's what it is."

After a moment, his white smile flashed in the dim evening light. "And now, my beautiful tourist..."

He assumed a firm tour guide stance and gestured so broadly that nearby a dazed British tour group turned to listen. "There by the entrance to Mandraki Harbor are the bronze deer on the great columns—the emblem of Rhodes." For several minutes he continued his detailed history lesson, then stopped and grinned at her. "How am I doing?"

Anne Marie laughed. "Very well. Although if you ever apply for guide work, you'll have to be more diplomatic about the Turks."

He chuckled. "Then I would never make it."

"And you've forgotten about the Colossus," she reminded him, "merely one of the Seven Wonders of the Ancient World."

He cleared his voice and assumed his tour guide stance again. "Overlooking this harbor was the Colossus, made of bronze and over one-hundred-feet tall!"

Affably nodding to the gaping tourists, he moved on with Anne Marie. "And how do you happen to know about the Colossus?"

"I read the ship's daily literature faithfully, but it didn't say how the Colossus disappeared."

"Earthquake," he answered. "Greece is a land of many earthquakes. Please make a note of that, Miss Gardene, to add to the ship's literature." He let loose with his hearty Greek laugh as they moved on. "I can imagine adding that to my list of recommendations to improve the *Golden Isle*'s service. Perhaps the writer's head would roll."

"Likely," Anne Marie agreed, smiling herself.

Later, as they walked through the narrow streets of the old town, he continued the amusing tour guide role, pointing out the museum—once the Knights of St. John's hospital—the medieval French and Spanish inns, the Grand Master's Palace.

Peering into the courtyards along the way, they saw profusions of flowers by the winding stairs that led to second-floor apartments. A splendid coat of arms hung over nearly every doorway, identifying the knight who had been in residence.

As they strolled along, the fragrance of jasmine hung in the night air. The evening held a softness, and slowly the rift between them seemed to be healing; it was as if the wonder of this medieval place reconciled their differences.

Anne Marie gazed up at the stars sparkling so high above the medieval city; the same stars had winked down on this place long before knights or medieval walls had even been considered. A surge of tenderness overcame her. "Thank you so much for showing me Rhodes, Alex. It's wonderful."

He slowly gathered her into his arms.

With the towers and battlements of the medieval city wall glowing behind him, he might have been a knight of old, taking his fair lady into his arms. His breath was warm and intimate as it brushed her face. "I've searched and searched, and I see it now. I've never met anyone else like you."

She smiled up into his eyes. There was a new bond, a new connection there. There would never be another rift between them again, she thought.

"No other woman has affected me like you do. From the first day I saw you when we were so young—to that day at Delphi, where it seemed that the gods blessed us—and now here, you make me so happy."

Her own heart overflowed.

"When I left the ship at Crete," he said, "I was furious. No other woman has run out on me, the heir to the Andropoulos fortune. But when I brought you to my cabin—when you ran away—I was not only insulted but actually stunned."

"Alex—"

"Please let me finish," he said, holding her head gently

against his shoulder. "From Crete I flew back to my old haunts with the jet set in Athens. I was so furious that I went where women wouldn't turn me down."

She began to pull away, but he held her firmly.

"You will be glad to hear that I saw the women there with new eyes. I wanted nothing to do with them. I couldn't eat, I couldn't sleep—" He drew a long breath. "When I came to my senses, I sent the fax, hoping it wasn't too late, hoping Jon hadn't stepped in and stolen you away. Am I too late?"

She shook her head. "No, it's not too late."

He lifted her off her feet joyously, and she thought he might have kissed her if they weren't surrounded by tourists.

It took a moment before he could summon up his tour guide tone again. "And now, my beautiful tourist, to Odos Sokratous Street, which—as the ads say—has been a bargain hunter's paradise since the fourteenth century!"

In the shops, Alex insisted on buying her an inexpensive, wide-brimmed, crocheted white hat to make amends. As she gave in, though, she recalled his buying her the white silk dress in Itea. The memory saddened her.

"Something wrong?" He placed the hat on her head at a chic angle.

"I'm afraid I'm a little tired. I shouldn't have skipped dinner; it makes me tire more quickly. The truth is that I couldn't eat or sleep well, either."

"I'm sorry to have hurt you, my sweet Anne Marie. Let's stop at that taverna to get something for you to eat."

Weaving through the groups of tourists, he led her to a nearby outdoor restaurant under a huge sprawling tree. Colorful lights strung along the branches brightened the darkness, and it was pleasant to sit down at one of the small wooden tables.

She settled back while Alex ordered a white wine for himself and a feta salad and lemonade for her. As they waited for their order, they watched the tourists pass by.

She smiled up at him coquettishly. "You look like king of all you survey."

"A medieval king of Rhodes?" He raised an amused eyebrow. "As long as all I survey includes you."

He slipped an arm around her shoulders and pulled her to him for an instant. To her surprise, instead of enjoying his embrace, she found herself hoping that Jon was not among the passing tourists.

As she finished her salad, Alex asked, "Are you strengthened now for the casino?"

"The casino? We're going to the casino?"

"Why not? Don't tell me that your faith doesn't let you go to a casino."

"My faith?" She made herself answer evenly. "My faith or lack of it has nothing to do with it, Alex. But I think you've been planning to go there all of this time."

He smiled. "I hoped so."

Certainly it was fair, but why hadn't he told her this was part of the bargain? Why had he assumed she'd want to go to a casino or even enjoyed gambling for that matter? Again, he'd leaped to a conclusion without asking, and the fact of the matter was that she didn't like gambling, or his...deviousness. Suddenly she remembered Lila's "See you later."

"There'll be taxis in the next street."

"I'm tired," she found herself protesting quite honestly. "I'd rather we went back to the ship."

He looked annoyed, then forced a smile. "Fine. I'll call a taxi for you."

"But I didn't mean—"

"Why not?" he interrupted. "You go to the ship for a good night's sleep, and I go to the casino. It's a fair exchange."

Her heart sank, but she was truly exhausted. "All right."

He hailed a taxi and opened the door for her. Smiling, he said, "See you in the morning."

He closed the door, still smiling, and spoke in Greek to the driver, then handed him several bills. Alex turned and gazed at her happily through the open window. "Let's meet on the dock at eight tomorrow morning."

As the taxi pulled away, he blew her a kiss. She nodded pleasantly, but his blown kiss and her farewell smile struck her as empty gestures.

Her disappointment lingered during the short ride back to the *Golden Isle*. How naive and trusting and...stupid she'd been. It was one thing that he'd expected to go to the casino all along, but another that Lila Thornton would be there, undoubtedly laughing at Anne Marie Gardene's foolishness once again.

At eight the next morning, Anne Marie was surprised to find Lila and Averill dozing in the taxi Alex had hired to take them to the village of Lindos on Rhodes' eastern shore. After their night at the casino, the Thorntons' presence was unexpected. Alex made no mention of what had happened the night before, and Anne Marie decided not to introduce the subject.

As he held the taxi door open for her, she noticed that Lila wore a provocatively cut black sundress and a glorious tan. By comparison, she felt like a schoolgirl in her pale, yellow cotton blouse and knee-length white shorts. Because of the heat, she'd pulled her hair back into a ponytail, which also paled considerably in comparison to Lila's magnificent auburn hair in a french twist.

"Good morning," she said, then slid into the middle of the back seat beside Lila.

Lila, her head reclining against the back of the seat, peered at Anne Marie through her thick black lashes, then closed her eyes again.

Averill only replied, "Good morning. Don't ask."

Alex settled beside Anne Marie and spoke in Greek to the driver, apparently something akin to "Let's see how fast you can make it to Lindos!"

The cab shot forward, tires screeching, and Anne Marie held onto the seat with alarm. "Another risk taker!"

Alex gave a laugh and slipped his arm around her shoulders. "Another Greek. Now sit back and don't worry. It's a point of honor with taxi drivers here to beat the tour buses to Lindos."

"I'm not surprised about that!"

Alex gave her shoulder a squeeze. "It appears this driver will not accept that disgrace."

She noticed the tour buses huffing away from the parking area near the *Golden Isle*; one of the buses carrying the Santa Rosita group was in front of them.

Just outside the city, their cab driver pulled out around the bus, determined to pass on the winding two-lane coastal highway. Terrified, Anne Marie caught her breath, then saw at the last moment that the road ahead was clear.

As they raced around the bus, she wondered if Jon was on it but refused to look. If Beth and Efrem saw how this taxi driver passed, they'd surely be praying for her.

Alex sat back unperturbed. "The entire town of Lindos has been designated as an archaeological site," he explained. "No other Acropolis in the world has so much to show, except ours in Athens, of course."

Although Lila's eyes remained closed, she spoke up. "Unfortunately that only means Averill must examine all of the Lindos excavations for the hundredth time."

Averill remained silent in the front seat where his narrow

head nodded occasionally in sleep, but Anne Marie wondered at his avid interest in archaeological sites. It seemed more than a dilettante's dabbling. He already had money and a stunning young wife. What did he seek in archaeology? What more did he want from life?

As they rode along, looking down on the sparsely inhabited blue Aegean coast, Anne Marie tried to ignore the Thorntons' presence. She smiled at Alex as she recalled the joyous beginning of their time last night in Rhodes.

His answering smile made his feelings clear. His hand cupped her shoulder, drawing her closer. Words were unnecessary as they looked out at the sea edging the wild coastline. Despite Anne Marie's doubts, he had returned to her.

White-washed villages in the typical Greek cubist style came into view. One village boasted a charming castle, and she thought how lovely it would be to live in such a village with Alex. If they married, it would be wonderful to stay here when they wanted to retreat from Athens. Surely a house here would not be too expensive.

"What are you looking so pleased about?" Alex whispered.

"Was I looking pleased?"

"Very," he returned. "And I am, too."

Her heart glowed with happiness, but when she turned from him, an unpleasant thought intruded. He had mentioned no plans for when the cruise ended.

"That's a monastery on the mountaintop," he remarked. "As far into history as we know, barren women have climbed the mountainside here to touch a miraculous icon so they might have children."

"And it worked for them?"

"Apparently," he answered. "It's said that women still make the climb."

She wondered if Alex would want children. His family

would likely expect future heirs for the shipping line. It suited her perfectly, though it wouldn't be the family she'd dreamed of to fill Aunt Sylvia's house. "Do you really think an icon can cause miracles?"

He chuckled. "I think perhaps it helps some women to overcome psychological problems."

"And it's not a miracle?"

He shrugged. "I believe only in what I can see, and sometimes not even all of that. I'm not a man who believes in miracles."

"You have faith only in yourself?"

"Yes."

"It's a limiting philosophy."

He nodded. "It is."

Later the cab dropped them off in the white-washed town of Lindos, where white buildings climbed the steep hillside to the old Acropolis.

"Let's ride the donkeys to the top," Alex suggested with enthusiasm. He led them to a row of donkey-owners who eagerly awaited tourists. "It's not a proper outing without riding a donkey to the top."

"I've never ridden a donkey," Anne Marie said hesitantly.

"All the more reason to do so," he answered. "It's easier than riding a horse or a camel. Here, this gray donkey looks docile enough."

Grateful to have worn knee-length shorts, Anne Marie climbed onto the animal with some trepidation. Instead of reacting, he seemed asleep on his feet.

Holding the reins, she glanced at Averill and bit back a smile. He was a comical sight with his long legs hanging over a donkey, his feet nearly touching the ground. Lila hiked up her black sundress, displaying beautifully tanned legs. "This is going to scratch hideously."

"You should have worn slacks," Alex told her. "You ought to know by now." He swung up onto a larger brown donkey and urged it forward in Greek. The donkey trotted off obediently. "A Greek donkey," he joked to everyone's amusement.

The guide led Anne Marie's donkey up the cobblestone promenade behind Alex's mount. Once she was accustomed to the animal's slow, steady gait, the *clip-clop* of its hooves on the pavement seemed an appropriate sound to accompany the magnificent vistas of curving coves and peninsulas jutting out into the bright blue Aegean.

Nearing the Acropolis at the top of the hill, they climbed off the donkeys, and Alex paid the guides. "We can walk down through the village on the way back. It's an old Greek maxim that downhill is easier."

"Not for me," Lila announced. "I like upward climbing."

"Indeed you do," Averill answered.

Anne Marie had the impression that he referred to more than hillside climbing, but Lila only raised her chin with amusement.

At the ruins, Averill took pleasure in sharing his knowledge. He went on and on about the colonnade, then the temple of Athena. Smiling, Alex reached for Anne Marie's hand. As he turned to go on, she felt Lila's stare and glanced back at her.

"Fool!" Lila mouthed.

Anne Marie quickly looked away, her heart pounding. What did the woman mean?

"The history of the entire island is contained in these ruins," Averill said and moved on.

Lila applied tanning lotion, ignoring her husband's explanation of the Byzantine church ruins, the castle of the Knights, and the Turkish fortifications. After a while she pronounced, "I'm going shopping."

"Again?" Averill asked with exasperation.

"They are what you call a complementary couple," Alex remarked dryly. "Entirely different interests."

"And where do your interests lie, Alex?" Lila asked, her German accent thick, her gray eyes smoldering.

"In the middle," Alex laughed. "Precisely in the middle."

"So! I'll remember that!" she flung her head back and made her departure.

"You're becoming a diplomat, Alex," Averill remarked.

"My father would be pleased to hear it from you," Alex replied.

He slipped his arm around Anne Marie's shoulders.

"Let's allow our friend Averill to enjoy the ruins in peace," he suggested, and they strolled away.

She felt uneasy. "Did I do something—"

Alex shook his head. "Forget it. Their troubles have nothing to do with us."

Although other tourists climbed through the ruins with them, it felt as if they were alone together in the warm sunshine. Walking out to a viewpoint, they saw St. Paul's Bay and the small white chapel built by the bay in his honor. Admiring the view, Anne Marie said, "Efrem told us that even now Greek dances and festivals take place there to celebrate the apostle Paul's visit to the bay."

"Yes, I've read about it," Alex replied. "We Greeks will dance and hold festivals for anything."

As they stood there, Efrem's group arrived on the hillside of the Acropolis. There were Beth and Jon—

"I want to take pictures," Anne Marie said, grabbing the camera that dangled from her neck so Alex had to remove his arm from her shoulders. *Why should I feel guilty to have Jon see me with Alex?* she asked herself.

Clicking one picture of St. Paul's Bay after another, she wished Alex would discuss their relationship. They only had today, tomorrow at sea, and a day in Egypt before he flew to Athens. If he loved her, wouldn't he have planned something for when the cruise ended?

CHAPTER

Eleven

After an elegant lunch in the *Golden Isle*'s dining room with Alex and Averill, Anne Marie made her way down the corridor of the Aegean Deck to her cabin. Lindos had been amazingly beautiful, as had the daylight walk through the medieval city of Rhodes, but already the island of Rhodes lay far behind them.

She opened the cabin door and saw Beth sitting on her bed, near tears again.

"What is it?" Anne Marie asked. "What's wrong?"

Beth pressed her lips together. "It's so difficult to forever pretend that...Efrem and I only have a platonic relationship. It's different at home, but here we're constantly together among so many church members, and they all seem to have differing views about remarriage for him."

"Does Efrem know it bothers you?"

Beth shook her head. "I...can't tell him."

"I think you're going to have to."

Tears filled Beth's eyes. "And cause trouble in the church? No way! Never!"

"They love you," Anne Marie assured her. "You care about

people. You're a loving woman. You spread kindness everywhere you go."

Beth shook her head again.

Anne Marie pressed on. "I've never felt so close to anyone as I have to you in such a short time. People can't help loving you, you're so full of love and enthusiasm. You, of all people, shouldn't have to berate yourself."

Beth blew her nose. "Thank you, but I'm so far from perfect that—"

"You're going to have to tell Efrem before you explode," Anne Marie told her quietly.

"But how? And what if he changes his mind about me?"

"If he changes his mind about you! Of all ideas! How can you even think it when it's so obvious that he loves you?"

"It is?" Beth asked.

Anne Marie nodded. It occurred to her that if Beth was unsure about a man who obviously loved her, perhaps every woman was unsure of a man's love until he actually married her. She considered her own uncertainty about Alex. He'd said that he loved her, but nothing else—nothing about total commitment. And now, oddly enough, Beth wondered about the same situation.

"I have an enormous favor to ask," Beth said. "I can't talk to Efrem in a public place. Would you please bring him here to the cabin? And could you stay with us here so people won't gossip?"

"You mean as a chaperone?"

Beth nodded. "As a chaperone."

Anne Marie hesitated. "The last time I acted as an intermediary in a romance, it was an unqualified disaster. I swore never to get involved again."

"Please..."

Anne Marie hesitated, then drew a deep breath. "All right,

but I hope it doesn't do more damage than good. I suppose I'd better do it now, but only if you wash those tear streaks from your face."

"Thank you, dear roomie."

Anne Marie gave her a small smile. "I hope you'll be thanking me a month from now."

"I think I will," Beth answered.

Glancing in the dressing table mirror, Anne Marie smoothed her hair. "I'll be back in a moment. Whatever you do, don't change your mind now."

In the corridor, several of the Santa Rosita group were headed in the other direction. She said a quick but fervent prayer for Beth and Efrem, then knocked on the neighboring cabin door.

Jon opened the door. "Hello! To what do we owe this honor?"

"I need to talk to Efrem."

Jon's surprise turned to concern, and seconds later Efrem arrived at the door. "What is it? Is something wrong?"

Anne Marie nodded. "Can you come to the cabin to see Beth? She's been crying."

He looked at her strangely, and she added, "She asked me to come back with you."

Efrem grabbed a cabin key from the ledge by his door. "See you later," he told Jon.

Neither of them spoke in the corridor, nor as she opened her cabin door. Inside, Beth sat on the bed and looked past her at Efrem in bewilderment.

Efrem hurried to her. "Beth, dear, what is it?"

"Oh, Efrem, it's so complicated..."

"Nothing is too complicated for God to fix," he said and Beth rose and threw her arms around him.

"Excuse me," Anne Marie said and exited into the bathroom. Surely her services at such close range were not required.

In the bathroom, she decided it was a good time to wash her hair. She could hear Beth sobbing again and Efrem trying to soothe her; a shower would drown out their voices.

Later, when she emerged from the bathroom with her hair washed and blown dry, Beth and Efrem were gone, and a note lie on her bed. *You're the first to be invited to our wedding this fall in Santa Rosita,* it said in Efrem's handwriting. *We'll be announcing the news soon.*

It was signed by both of them, and Beth had added *JOY!!!!!*

Anne Marie's heart leapt with happiness for them. If only her life were settled too.

Climbing the steps to the Sun Deck, Anne Marie wished that Alex had suggested an activity for this afternoon. Still, she could sun herself and read the new novel she had purchased in the ship's gift shop just minutes ago.

When she arrived at the topmost deck the sea of chaise lounges was already crowded with sunbathers, most of them reading or asleep. The blinding light made her momentarily uncertain of the man sleeping in a distant yellow lounge.

Alex? Indeed it was!

She swallowed with dismay as she realized the woman in the chaise beside his was Lila, wearing a skimpy black bikini.

As their eyes met, Lila's lips curled up smugly, and Anne Marie decided it was too late to retreat. There was nothing to do except make her way through the tangle of sunbathers in her sedate white terry cloth cover-up that covered her equally sedate turquoise bathing suit. Pressing her lips together, she headed for the only empty chaises and finally settled on a yellow lounge several rows in front of them.

Rubbing sunblock on her legs, she tried to recall exactly what Alex had said about this afternoon. Only that he had work to do and then he was going to rest. Perhaps Lila had invited herself. It wouldn't be surprising.

She pondered Alex and Lila's relationship. They were obviously old friends. At lunch, it had become completely clear that Averill was part of a banking consortium that loaned money to the Andropoulos shipping line, so it made sense that Alex had to keep them happy. But how did Lila fit into it? Surely Alex wasn't required to be quite so friendly with her.

Anne Marie tried to read the novel, but her mind skimmed the words absently as she mulled over her situation. Overhead the ship's smokestack roared and hissed, its sound blending into the symphony of the sea. The sun warmed her body and, after a while, she rolled over, wishing she could sleep, wishing she could stop her suspicions.

Her tension drained away slowly, and her mind drifted back to the moments in the ancient stadium of Delphi, and then into sleep.

"Oh, Alex," she whispered in her dream as he drew her into his arms.

They moved now to the moonlit streets of Rhodes, the towers and battlements of the medieval walls behind him. She'd never felt such bliss, but slowly something began to intrude, something intent on ripping them apart. In the shadows behind Alex was the laughing face of Lila Thornton.

"Fool!" Lila said. "Fool!"

Much later, Anne Marie awakened, smelling sea air and tasting the faint flavor of salt on her lips. Sitting up, she realized where she was. Her arms, legs, and back glowed with the sun's heat, though the air wasn't nearly as hot as when she'd arrived on deck. She darted a look toward the chaises where Alex and Lila had been sitting.

Empty.

In her cabin, she found the telephone light glowing and

phoned the operator for her message.

"Call Alex," he said.

She put the call through with trepidation, but Alex sounded as if nothing had changed, as if he was delighted to hear her voice. "I'm having a working dinner with the captain and several of the ship's officers in the captain's quarters tonight," he apologized. "Sorry. We'll be talking late, so I can't see you."

She decided to trust him. "Of course, Alex. I understand. Don't worry about me. I know you're inspecting the ship."

"Tomorrow we'll have the entire day together," he promised.

"Marvelous." Her spirits lifted so quickly that she heard the smile in her voice. Their day together tomorrow would make up for not seeing him tonight or being with him this afternoon.

As she hung up, she decided not to dress for dinner. She'd get a salad and pizza at the ship's grill rather than face everyone—and their questions—at the Santa Rosita tables.

The next morning, Anne Marie awakened so early that she decided to have breakfast in the dining room for a change. Beth still slept, and happy as she was for her, she did not care to face her cabinmate's joyful face. Nor did she wish to encounter Jon, who usually ate out on the Promenade Deck.

Dressed, she closed the cabin door softly, headed down the quiet corridor, then down in the elevator for the dining room.

As she made her way to their usual table, she was amazed to see Jon sitting at it alone. Worse, he'd seen her, as had their waiter who was making a lavish show of rushing over to pull a chair out for her.

From the corner of her eye, she noticed the maitre d' and the waiters exchanging looks, most likely wondering what had happened between her and their employer, Alex.

"Good morning." Jon set down his cup of coffee and rose to

his feet. "I didn't expect to see you here this morning."

She managed a smile, wondering if he'd hoped to avoid her, too. "Good morning."

Thanking the waiter for the breakfast menu, she then turned to Jon. "Where is everyone?"

"Efrem's still asleep."

"So is Beth."

He grinned. "The newlyweds-to-be were up late, discussing wedding plans, I presume."

"Then you know, too." She opened her menu. "Have they told anyone else?"

"Just us, I think." He chuckled. "It's fierce being cabinmates with a fifty-five-year-old man in love. I'm surprised he hasn't shouted their engagement over the ship's public address system. That's what I'd—"

Suddenly his color deepened, and apparently he saw someone, for he rose to his feet again.

Anne Marie turned to find the Nathans and Williamsons arriving at the table. She wondered just what it was that Jon thought he would do and she wished he hadn't been interrupted.

Nat Nathan smiled to see them. "Well, if this isn't the best showing we've had here at breakfast since the cruise began! All we need now is Efrem and Beth to fill the table."

"Beth's still asleep," Anne Marie answered, then quickly stared into her menu.

"They must have been up late," Kate Nathan remarked. "I pray they don't jump into something they'll regret. We've seen so many couples make mistakes in their second marriages. It's as if some couples would do anything to stop the loneliness, and then they're stuck with a mistake and a new kind of misery."

Newlywed Reynold Williamson chuckled. "Frankly speaking, they seem a little too sensible to me."

His wife, Rena, raised her hands to halt the subject. "It's God's business, not ours—"

"Ours, too, as long as we're members of the church," Nat put in. "God allows us all to make mistakes, sometimes because we're not listening to him. We'd be remiss if we didn't slow them down a little."

Fortunately the waiter arrived to take breakfast orders, then the busboy came with orange juice and coffee.

Once the servers left the table, Kate Nathan said again, "We don't want them rushing into anything."

Rena said, "We only knew each other six months before we married, and I couldn't be happier. Nat, would you like to say grace?"

Beth and Efrem did have ample reason to be circumspect, Anne Marie thought as Nat gave thanks. Likely these two otherwise lovely couples saw romantic matters so differently because the Nathans had been married forever and the Reynolds were second-time newlyweds themselves.

As they began to eat, Rena quickly turned the conversation to their leisurely day at sea and the next day's visit to Egypt.

"Seeing the pyramids will be such a thrill," Mrs. Nathan said. "Why, I remember studying about them when I was a schoolgirl."

All in all, it turned out to be a pleasant breakfast—and nothing was mentioned about Anne Marie and Alex.

She and Jon left the table together and were at the dining room door when Alex appeared before them. "There you are!" he exclaimed. "I thought maybe you'd jumped ship."

Anne Marie smiled. "Were you looking for me?"

"I telephoned and only managed to awaken your cabinmate, who had no idea you were up and gone. How would you like to meet on the Sun Deck at ten? I'll bring along my paperwork, and we can get some sun."

She was aware of Jon standing nearby, but decided to do

what her heart dictated. "It sounds like a lovely idea, Alex."

"See you then," he said.

The maitre d' had already rushed forward to greet Alex, and now stood back deferentially, waiting for him to finish his conversation. Other waiters watched, too.

"See you at ten," Alex said.

"Yes," she answered. "At ten."

Before Jon could ask questions, she excused herself and darted off toward the nearby ladies room.

"See you later," she called back to him.

At ten o'clock she climbed the stairs to the Sun Deck again, pondering whether she was the fool Lila claimed her to be. On the deck, she saw Alex already settling down on the very chaise where he had lounged next to Lila the day before.

He looked up as if sensing Anne Marie's gaze, then drank in every movement as she approached.

"Is this your private chaise?" she couldn't help asking.

"No, but it's in the best place to avoid being spattered by droplets of oil from the smokestack. Come, sit down. You know, Anne Marie Gardene, you are surely the most beautiful woman on the ship."

She laughed. "Only because blonds are so rare in Greece. And don't you remember that my mother used to say that only fools are taken in by flattery?"

"Are you a fool?"

She shrugged lightly.

Shedding her terry cloth cover-up, she felt his lingering scrutiny. Probably he found her too old-fashioned in her one-piece bathing suit.

"Today is ours," he said. "There's nothing to do except relax, and I sorely need it."

"Where are the Thorntons?" she asked, then wished that she'd held her tongue. It almost appeared that he was splitting his days evenly between her and Lila.

"Averill is sick. They've had the ship's doctor up to their suite."

"I'm sorry to hear it." She did like Averill, though she pitied him as Lila's husband. "His heart again?"

"Apparently. The doctor told Lila to stay nearby to keep him quiet and to give him his medicine."

Anne Marie couldn't imagine Lila's reaction to such an edict, but perhaps she'd misjudged the woman.

She dug the plastic bottle of sunblock from her beachbag and slowly rubbed the white liquid onto her already tan arms and legs.

"Do you want me to put lotion on your back?" Alex offered.

"No, thank you." He no doubt had performed that rite for Lila yesterday.

"Something is wrong," Alex guessed. Before she knew what had happened, he snatched the plastic bottle of lotion from her. "All right now, my lovely tourist, roll over. I'm going to rub this on your back, and you're going to tell me what's troubling you."

She rolled over, mainly to avoid his gaze. Lila had been on this very chaise yesterday. How could she not help being suspicious and jealous? Tears stung her eyes, but Alex's warm hand moved across her back, slowly smoothing the lotion on her, soothing her tension away. After a while, she was certain that he'd finished, but she made no attempt to stop his hand.

"Now, let's hear what is wrong."

She absolutely would not tell him.

"Anne Marie?" he whispered into her hair. "Please tell me what is wrong."

Please? It didn't strike her as a word in his vocabulary.

He lifted her hair and softly whispered, "Please tell me."

"It's just that—" She stopped, then blurted, "It's just that I don't know if you really care for me."

The silence between them hung so heavily that she finally glanced up into his reflective sunglasses, where she only saw her own image.

"Of course I care for you," he said and helped her to sit up. He cupped her chin in his hand. "Of course I care," he repeated, filling her heart with happiness. He seemed unaware of the other sunbathers around them. "I wanted to talk to you about it today," he added. "I'd like for you to spend a month or so with me in Athens after the cruise. I, too, feel we should know each other better. It's been so many years—"

His family must have approved of her. How could she have doubted? She would give up her teaching job...

"You still remind me of Anna—of her loving innocence. There's not much of that left in the world."

"Oh, Alex!" she protested.

But hope and happiness surged through her veins again, and the remainder of the day seemed to brim with a glorious light as together they ate lunch, toured the ship's bridge, and held hands during the humorous afternoon movie.

Afterward, they lolled on the deck, reminiscing about his stay in Nebraska and discussing the ports of call ahead in Egypt and Israel. Alex would be flying from Cairo back to Athens for business appointments made months ago. He would have to skip Israel entirely, but he'd be waiting for her at the dock in Greece, and that would be the beginning of their new life together.

He'd mentioned nothing about marriage, but that would come—after all, a man wouldn't invite a woman to stay with his family for such a length of time unless his intentions were serious, especially not in Greece where traditions like marriage were apparently still taken seriously.

In the evening they dined at a romantic candlelit table for

two, then sat out on the Promenade Deck in the starlight as the ship sailed across the dark Mediterranean Sea.

The *Golden Isle* had slowed when she awakened the next morning, and Beth was already dressed. Seeing Anne Marie awake, she leaned over the bed to look out their porthole. "Hey, it's Egypt! We're really going to Egypt! And there's a big lineup of ships probably bound for the Suez Canal."

Anne Marie's eyes opened wide, and she kneeled on her bed to gaze out the porthole herself. Sunshine gleamed through gray clouds, scattering rays of pink and gold across the sky and gilding the silvery gray sea. There was indeed a lineup of ships, and far in the distance, the city of Port Said.

"I'm going out," Beth said excitedly. "See you later!"

Anne Marie was tempted to tell her that Alex had invited her to stay with his family after the cruise, but Beth had already closed the cabin door behind her.

When Anne Marie stepped outside on the Aegean Deck, a minuscule tug encircled by black tires was approaching the *Golden Isle*. She hurried down to the Promenade Deck and looked for Alex. No sign of him. Instead, she spotted Beth with Efrem, and Jon tagging along.

Beth and Efrem seemed too caught up in the magnificent pink-and-gold sunrise to notice her, but Jon turned and grinned. "There's our sleepyhead!"

"It's not even six o'clock yet," she protested, "but it's worth getting up for this sunrise."

"Yes, it is," Jon answered. After a moment, he added, "You look just as sleepy-eyed as when you were a girl and we went fishing in the morning."

The brightness of his blue eyes was startling in the morning light. "Do you really remember those mornings?"

"Of course I do," he replied. "I even remember one morning on the rowboat when I braided your hair."

"You remember that?"

"Don't you?"

She nodded. "Yes, I remember."

"It was a half-brained thing to do," he said, "but I've never forgotten."

"I didn't think it was so half-brained. In fact, I'm still glad you did it."

"You are?"

"I am." For years, she'd remembered it all too well, she thought as she turned with him to watch the tug hook up to the *Golden Isle.* Probably he'd never even suspected how golden those moments had been for her.

As the ship neared Port Said, the city was actually gray and shabby—a disappointment after seeing it shimmering in the distance earlier. She looked around the deck for Alex. No sign of him.

Settling down at an outdoor table with their orange juice and croissants, she and Jon watched the approach to Port Said. The harbor bustled with activity: great container ships flying red, white, and black Egyptian flags; rusty barges carrying burlap-wrapped bales of cotton; an exotic green ferry passing with its men all waving like children. On the nearest bank, a gray-haired hansom cab driver dropped his old horse's reins to stand up and wave vigorously with both hands in the air, then dipped a grandiose bow of welcome.

Anne Marie joined in the festivities, waving back with the other passengers.

Suddenly Alex was beside her with an exuberant, "There you are! How beautiful you look!"

"Only because I'm excited to be in Egypt."

She was pleased she'd worn her hair in a Grecian fall and

chosen a white cotton blouse and culottes for camel riding.

He smiled wryly. "I suppose you've been up since dawn."

"I have, and I'm glad of it."

He laughed, then turned to shake hands with Jon, who seemed to have paled under his tan. Next, she introduced Alex to Beth and Efrem, who smiled and shook hands politely with him. Seconds later, Lila appeared in a thin-strapped green jersey dress, and Anne Marie felt herself grow tense. No, she would not allow Lila to affect her like this.

Lila told Alex, "I'm going ashore. The doctor says there's no reason for me to stay aboard."

"Then Averill must be feeling better," Alex replied, his voice even.

"Much better," Lila answered. "Climbing around on the ruins wears him out, that's all."

Anne Marie looked away quickly, trying not to read anything into the exchange between Alex and Lila. But why, oh, why, didn't Lila stay aboard with her husband? And why didn't she stay away from Alex? Couldn't the woman see she wasn't wanted? Or was that precisely why she intruded?

They moved along with the throng of passengers heading for the gangway as the ship approached the dock. Far below in the water, vendors in rowboats waved their wares.

"Camel saddle, lady?" Alex joked with her. "A fine red plastic suitcase?"

"A tooled plastic wallet, sir?" she tossed back at him.

In the press of the crowd, Lila turned to Jon with an inviting smile. "I hope you'll join us in the limo Alex has rented for the drive to Cairo. Averill can't go today, and you're such good company. It would be so much more pleasant for you than riding in a tour bus."

Anne Marie felt her heart sink as Jon looked at her for approval. "Yes, why don't you?" she felt obliged to say, then was furious with both herself and Lila. This was Alex's last day on the ship—the last day she'd have with him until she returned to Athens at the end of the cruise!

Alex nodded cordially at Jon. "We would be pleased to have you join us. Two men would be better than one to ward off the Egyptian men's interest in these ladies. They especially like blonds and redheads."

Lila laughed. "We need your protection, Jon."

"I'm honored," he replied with amusement.

Best to be pleasant about the matter instead of letting it ruin their day in Egypt, Anne Marie decided, then headed for the disembarkation doorway.

The Egyptians had towed a pontoon dock with a narrow metal bridge to the ship, and before long, Anne Marie balanced precariously on the metal bridge over the water to the dock. Vendors in rowboats and on the shore called out to the disembarking passengers. On the dock, white-uniformed Egyptian officials lined the broken sidewalk to the street like an honor guard. Beyond them, a black-uniformed limousine driver waited for Alex with a ship's officer.

"If you please," the driver said. He whisked Alex, Lila, Jon, and Anne Marie through the throng of enthusiastic vendors who wore tattered robes and dingy white turbans.

Opening the limousine's doors, the driver cast curious glances at the four of them to see who was with whom. Even he sensed their peculiar situation, Anne Marie thought.

"Jon, why don't you take the middle seat with Lila," Alex suggested.

Anne Marie was glad to hear it and equally glad that Jon helped Lila in with no comment.

Driving through the Egyptian countryside, the driver, Mohammed, spoke in heavily-accented English, pointing out the nearby ships in the Suez Canal. The canal and its water were too low to be visible, and the tops of cargo ships, tankers, and dredges appeared to be driving along a road just over the adjacent strip of land.

At the sound of a police siren, then the sight of a police car blinking its emergency lights, Mohammed said, "Ah, here come the tour buses." He swung the limousine into the right-hand lane. "They are allowed to drive faster than anyone else nowadays."

Indeed, the convoy of fifteen new tour buses rode past them with dispatch in the fast lane, followed by a military truck that held seven or eight soldiers with machine guns.

"What's that about?" Anne Marie asked.

"The fundamentalists shot some tourists not too long ago, and Egypt values its tourist income, not to mention the foreign aid from your country," Alex replied. He caught her hand and held it firmly in his. "Don't concern yourself about it. This is our last day together until you return to Athens."

"Yes, our last day."

He glanced out the car window on his side. "Look, the scene might be from the murals of ancient Egypt."

She gazed out with him at the pastoral sights. Farmers pushed such primitive plows that they might indeed have stepped from ancient Egypt. Mud huts with bright green wooden doors stood near flooded sections of land. It was a calming sight.

"Green is our holy color," Mohammed explained, then cast a glance at Lila's provocative, green, thin-strapped dress.

Anne Marie wondered if Lila had purposely worn it to cause a stir. After all, she and Averill traveled endlessly and had mentioned visiting other Muslim countries. In Turkey, women with bare upper arms or revealing necklines had not been allowed to tour the mosques; surely Lila knew the same rules must apply in Egypt.

Alex took such an interest in the sights that Anne Marie asked, "Haven't you ever been here?"

"Only to the Valley of the Kings years ago. Egypt is too primitive for Greeks," he added with a chuckle.

"And for a German," Lila agreed. "Averill, of course, has spent weeks among the ruins—without me!"

Anne Marie hoped the driver hadn't heard their disparaging remarks. Fortunately Jon had been speaking politely with him.

When they arrived in Cairo, they drove through the dusty, bustling city to the mosque. Lila smiled when she was not admitted because of her dress. "I'm content to sit in an air-conditioned limousine and watch the passing scene while you are searching for Allah," she laughed.

At lunchtime, they drove through the wild traffic to the elegant Nile Hilton. In its spacious dining room they ate shish kebab while an overweight belly dancer undulated to the sensuous music. Alex and Lila expressed their amusement, but Jon, after a noncommittal glance, kept his back to the stage. Anne Marie, for her part, decided she didn't care to see women exploited, either.

After lunch, they hurried across the street to the dusty but famous Cairo Museum to see the magnificent treasures of Tutankhamen and other pharaohs. Far too soon they were whisked out and driven through Cairo to the pyramids at Giza.

As the day progressed, Anne Marie grew more and more frustrated with Lila. Why had the woman come ashore? She wasn't interested in Egypt. She personified the old saying about tourists who returned home "with traveled bodies, but untraveled minds."

At the edge of Cairo, Mohammed pointed out the tan pyramids of Giza, which were suddenly upon them.

Lila groused, "And here we have the pyramids right in the city."

"They were once far from the city," Mohammed explained evenly. "The city has spread to here."

They climbed out of the limousine at the edge of the road, and mahogany-tanned boys ran to them shouting.

"Camel rides to the pyramids!"

"Camel rides!"

"Here is Egypt's best camel!"

The haughty-faced camels, wearing colorful tassels and saddle blankets, eyed them with disdain—*a bit like Lila,* Anne Marie thought, then felt guilty.

Jon had been quiet despite his obvious interest in sights. Now he said, "I'm going to fulfill a lifelong ambition and ride a camel."

"I'd never forgive myself if I missed this chance," Anne Marie decided, too.

"You crazy Americans!" Alex laughed. "Camels smell terrible. Terrible! What's worse, they bite!"

"My camel, he no bite!" protested an eager young camel guide. "He no bite!"

"Good, I'll take him," Anne Marie said to the delight of the dingy-robed camel boy. One whiff of the mangy animal's barnyard odor, and she knew why the camel's owner hadn't argued about their smell.

"Whew!" Jon said as he hired a camel himself.

Alex laughed. "Didn't I warn you? I suppose you'll want to go into the pyramid, too."

"Good idea," Jon answered as he climbed onto his camel. "I didn't know we could go in."

Behind them, Alex hired a horse and wagon for Lila and himself, then shouted, "We'll beat you to the pyramids!"

"I thought you were such a risk taker!" Anne Marie called after him as he and Lila walked to the wagon.

Looking back at her, he laughed again. "I choose my risks carefully nowadays."

She laughed with him. "So I see!"

The young guide helped her up onto the kneeling camel's saddle blanket, and she fought off a twinge of jealousy as Lila and Alex sat down on the wagon seat. Suddenly her camel jerked to his feet, and she nearly flew over the beast's head.

"Hang on!" Jon shouted.

"Now you tell me!" she groused, desperately gripping the saddle horn.

The guide walked alongside Anne Marie, holding the reins as the camel lumbered along the sandy road like a ship buffeted by wave after wave.

Anne Marie held on, certain she'd pitch over her camel's head if she didn't fall off on one side or the other.

"Well, if it isn't the Queen of Sheba!" Jon called over as his camel caught up with hers.

"And a desert sheik!" she teased back.

"It's an adventure," he answered. "I keep telling myself it's an adventure."

Once accustomed to the camel's pitch and sway, she thought it did feel rather regal to ride so high past the colorful tourist shops, then to the edges of the nearby desert. Alex and Lila were already halfway there in their horse and wagon.

At long last, the camels neared the three enormous pyramids. "I'll never forget this," she told Jon, whose camel now pitched and swayed alongside hers.

"Not likely that I will either!" he said, grinning like a boy. "Are you going into one of the pyramids?"

"I wouldn't miss it."

Her camel lowered himself, and she was relieved to get off the smelly beast—and for Jon to be there to give her a hand, too, even if he did hold it a trifle too long. She turned her attention to the pyramids.

At this close range, they took on a gray tone. The stone

blocks had deteriorated badly—their worn, darkened edges attesting to their age.

"I remember from Sunday school lessons that the Hebrew slaves built these pyramids for the great Egyptian pharaohs," she said. "Also that an Egyptian princess found Moses among the Nile's bulrushes. Here, it no longer seems a Bible story or an old legend, but a real possibility."

"It does," Jon answered. "I didn't know you went to Sunday school."

"I did."

They smiled again, and she knew this was not a discussion she was apt to have with Alex.

A new mahogany-colored guide named Ahmed followed her and Jon around to the open pyramid. "I take you down into pyramid." He coughed and spat, then blew his nose into his robe. "I take you down into pyramid," he repeated insistently.

She glanced around for another guide, but the other guides stood back; it was obviously Ahmed's turn, and five other tourists had joined them. At the pyramid's open doorway, she looked at Jon. "All right with you?"

"Let's go," he replied.

"You hold my hand," Ahmed told her.

Anne Marie took his hand with some reluctance, then followed him down the narrow stone steps into the pyramid. Jon held her other hand, and the five additional tourists trailed behind them. Almost immediately the sunlight disappeared from the passageway.

"I can't see!" Anne Marie called out in the darkness. "I can't see the steps! I can't see anything."

Behind her, Jon gripped her hand more tightly, and she was glad of it.

"Is okay!" Ahmed answered. "Hold hands! I see good. I see

good for all. Now we go up."

He urged them upward, step by step, into the pyramid, and it seemed they'd gone a mile when the steps stopped and they stood on the dirt floor of a large chamber lit by a single lantern and holding only a nondescript sarcophagus.

"I don't know what I expected," Anne Marie remarked. "Maybe an Indiana Jones scene. Not something so empty."

"It's not the treasures of Tutankhamen," Jon replied as they looked about the chamber, "but now we've been inside one of Egypt's pyramids."

"That we have," she agreed.

Later, Lila and Alex hung back by the limousine, content to view the sights from a distance. In front of the great stone Sphinx, Anne Marie and Jon stood together taking pictures, enjoying the zealous Egyptian vendors.

"They remind me of kindergartners bursting out for recess."

Jon laughed. "You'll have a new perspective—viewing your students as potential tourist guides and vendors."

"It's a thought!"

When they'd all returned to the limousine, Lila produced a card with the name of an exclusive shop in Cairo. "Now you see why I've come," she admitted happily. "My dressmaker says they have fabulous fabrics."

Alex laughed. "At least you are honest about it."

It was already dark when their limousine wove through the wild Cairo traffic, then roared back to the ship. Despite the exotic sights of Egypt, Anne Marie felt tired and oddly depressed, even with Alex's arm around her. The cruise had almost ended; only Israel remained. She'd quelled all thoughts of Alex leaving, but now reality awaited. He would leave in a few hours for Athens. If only they'd had this day together without Jon and Lila to complicate matters.

Alex pulled her to him as the limousine neared the dock at Port Said. "You're quiet."

She nodded, resting her head on his shoulder. "I don't want you to go."

He dropped a kiss on her forehead. "I don't want to leave you, either."

After a moment, he dug out his wallet. "Let me give you my personal card in case you have to reach me." He handed the embossed white card to her. "It's my private phone at the office, and here is my apartment number."

"Your apartment in Athens?" she inquired.

"Surely you didn't think I still lived at home with my parents?"

"I...I hadn't thought about it," she replied. "I assumed you lived with your family because that's where you took me."

A sudden thought struck Anne Marie. Had Alex meant she was invited to his apartment? Or was it to his parents' home? In an agony of confusion, she was afraid to ask.

The limousine stopped on the dock, and Mohammed let them out into the chaotic vendor scene by the *Golden Isle*'s gangway. *Now Alex will have to collect his luggage and a helicopter will take him to the Cairo airport,* Anne Marie thought. She felt like weeping.

In the ship's salon, Jon and Lila bade them good night, Jon's eyes flickering over Anne Marie unhappily as he left.

Trying to ignore Jon, Anne Marie asked Alex, "Must you really leave? Surely you can change your plans."

"I can't, but I'll see you in Athens," he responded. "And if I can't be there, I'll have the company limo waiting the moment the ship docks, and then you'll be with me. We'll have romantic evenings on the Greek islands and dancing in the tavernas."

Don't ask for trouble, she warned herself. *Don't ruin anything now.*

Yet, she had to know.

She forced the words out. "Will I be staying in your apartment or in your parents' home?"

He looked unnerved, his Adam's apple jumping, then suddenly irritated, as if it were improper to inquire. A crewman interrupted with Alex's luggage, and Alex dispatched him down the gangway with the suitcases.

"A kiss," Alex said, catching her in his arms.

She pulled away and asked again, "In your apartment or in your parents' home?"

Alex raised an annoyed eyebrow. "In my apartment, of course. We couldn't possibly go to my parents' house."

Her words tumbled out so rapidly she hardly knew she would say them. "You've never even considered marrying me!"

Stunned, he blurted, "Of course not. I have to marry a Greek girl like Marina Zafis, someone whose family's business is compatible with ours."

He stopped, but it was enough for her to remember the young girl at his parents' house, enough for her to understand: Alex was expected to marry someone whose family was wealthy and important in Greek industry. Perhaps he and his family had thought Marina's presence for lunch had made that entirely clear.

"You said you cared for me," Anne Marie whispered unsteadily.

"But I do!" He gripped her shoulders. "Didn't I come back to the ship for you? I've never done anything like that for another woman. You're different and refreshing—"

"And a virgin!" she interrupted. "You knew that."

"I assumed so," he replied. "It makes me all the happier and more grateful..."

"I suppose that has something to do with your choosing your risks carefully nowadays."

He nodded slightly. “I won’t lie. Yes, it’s a consideration, but it’s more than that.”

She looked into his intense, dark-eyed gaze. He wanted her on his own terms—which did not include marriage. There was something more foreign between them than their cultures—a difference in morals. She recalled her parents’ concern over her attraction to him, and the reputations of the girls he’d dated in Nebraska. Not to mention the question of Lila.

How differently she and Alex saw matters. Maybe it was her old Sunday school lessons from so long ago, or maybe it was her idealism about marriage. Whatever it was, it made a life with Alex impossible.

She looked hopelessly into his eyes. “I won’t be staying with you, Alex.”

“What?”

“I won’t be staying with you.”

“Don’t say that,” he pleaded, pulling her to him. “I’ll be waiting for you—”

“No!” she protested. “No!”

She tore away from him, and his eyes were incredulous. “No?”

“No,” she repeated, trembling. “Good-bye, Alex.”

She turned and ran toward the ship’s closest elevator.

Inside the elevator she stared blindly ahead, scarcely aware of it moving, scarcely remembering to step off on the Aegean Deck. So many years she’d dreamed of him…

Trembling, she hurried to her cabin. She fumbled in her handbag for her key and barely made it into the empty cabin before the ache in her heart gave way to sobbing.

CHAPTER

Twelve

The next morning Anne Marie awakened, still devastated. The ship had docked in Haifa sometime during the night, but her heartache dulled every vestige of excitement at being in Israel. She slipped out of bed and told Beth, "It's all over this time. It's all over with Alex."

Beth was already dressed and had been reading her Bible. She stood up and held her arms out to Anne Marie. "I'm sorry, so sorry. I'm not going to ask questions—nor pretend to have all the answers—but my heart goes out to you."

Anne Marie let her cabinmate hold her for an instant, then pulled away. "You're not going to remind me that God loves me?"

Beth shook her head. "I think someone's already told you. Likely your Aunt Sylvia."

"Yes. In any event, I give up on men forever. I'm sick and tired of them. I'll be glad to get back to school so I can forget them." She hoped Beth wouldn't say she'd pray for her. Probably she'd been praying for her all along.

Instead, Beth replied, "Can't say I blame you. Men can be troublesome, to put it mildly. I can imagine you with your kindergartners. I'd guess those little ones in your class are loved to pieces."

"I do love them," Anne Marie replied, heading for the bathroom. Fortunately she'd hung out a white T-shirt and culottes last night. She added her turquoise belt and silver earrings. Unfortunately, she felt more like wearing black for mourning.

As she brushed her teeth, she recalled Beth telling her earlier on the trip, "At least you have someone else who loves you. Can't you see that Jon Barnett is crazy about you?"

That was undoubtedly over, too. Last night she'd overheard the Nathans and Williamsons talking in the corridor. Kate Nathan had remarked, "Jon vowed he'd only marry someone who shared his beliefs."

Anne Marie told herself she wasn't interested in him anyhow, though his sharing-beliefs attitude seemed like another indictment. For Alex, she wasn't sufficiently immoral, and for Jon, she wasn't sufficiently spiritual. Well, she could manage without them. She'd manage no matter how deep her loneliness, and she'd enjoy these two days in Israel.

Dressed, she stepped from the bathroom and was glad Beth was already gone. It was even more difficult now to deal with her roommate's engagement.

She glanced at her watch, then grabbed her handbag. The buses would be leaving for Caesarea in minutes.

As she stepped out on the ship's gangway, several tour buses were already leaving the dock, but the two Santa Rosita buses still waited. Beth and Efrem stood at the open door of one bus, waving at her to hurry.

Anne Marie guessed Jon would be on the bus with them. "I'll take the other bus!" she called to Beth and ran for it.

Climbing the steps into the other bus, she was greeted with "Good mornings" and friendly faces, and hoped her unhappiness was not evident. At least Jon wasn't on this bus. She didn't need more of his disapproval. Finding an empty seat, she settled next to the window. Today she wanted to be alone, away from thoughts of Alex or Jon or anyone else.

As the bus pulled away, she stared blindly at the outskirts of Haifa, then at the sparkling Mediterranean. Despite her attempts to forget, memories of Alex surfaced and deepened her anguish.

At Caesarea, she hung back at the edge of the group as they surveyed the ruins of the Roman city built by Pontius Pilate. The setting, she had to agree, was memorable: the bright blue Mediterranean stretched out into the horizon and was fronted by ancient white ruins.

Far ahead, Efrem said, "We are walking on the remnants of a Roman road built over two thousand years ago. You can see where it was worn down by chariot wheels. It was also polished by the feet of centurions."

In the Roman amphitheater, the group settled on rows of dingy marble seats, and Anne Marie listened to Efrem as she looked out at the brilliant blue sea. She wondered if religion might somehow help her hurting heart, if it could help her to forget Alex, if it could still the pangs of loneliness.

"Jesus was never here in Caesarea to our knowledge," Efrem began, "but Paul surely was..."

Later, the bus headed inland from the Mediterranean coast and through the Valley of Sharon toward Jerusalem. Sitting alone, Anne Marie found herself vaguely missing Jon's company. He would be keenly interested in everything from the flowers and trees to the Roman ruins. Perhaps if Alex hadn't come on the cruise, things might have turned out differently.

The attractive tour bus guide, Etti, discussed the passing countryside in relationship to the Old and New Testaments and, after a while, Anne Marie's agony eased. Slowly, the shadowy film of the ages seemed to lift, and she visualized the great biblical battles. Her mind wandered into history. Surely thousands of other women with broken hearts had passed through these very places throughout the centuries.

Approaching Jerusalem, the land was green with young forests planted since the Jews had returned. Unfortunately, rusting armored cars stood as monuments to Israel's recent wars—and to more aching hearts besides hers.

As the bus rounded a curve, Anne Marie had her first view of Jerusalem, of sunstruck buildings climbing the hillsides.

"'And I…saw the holy city, new Jerusalem, coming down from God out of heaven,'" the tour guide read from the Book of Revelation. In her imagination, Anne Marie saw it descending, radiant with light, just above the old city.

Later, as the bus drove through the edge of Jerusalem, robed Arabs, Hassidic Jews in black coats and hats, and people in western clothing bustled along the dusty streets. White-washed apartment buildings rose against the blue sky, and here and there pink and white oleander bushes bloomed. They drove through the outskirts of Jerusalem, then turned away and drove through the countryside again.

"Here in the Judean hills, shepherds still tend their sheep," Etti said later. "Ahead is Bethlehem, the city of David."

Bethlehem!

Despite everything, Anne Marie marveled to see the old town spilling down a terraced hillside to fields where sheep grazed. From this distance, the scenery was just like she'd imagined it had been centuries ago.

"Rachel, wife of Jacob, was buried nearby," Etti continued. "Ruth and Naomi settled here. It is also the birthplace of David, the place where the prophet Micah foretold the birth of the Messiah would occur. Centuries later, a Roman census brought Mary and Joseph here."

On the hillside, a shepherd tended a flock of sheep. *A similar sight to that which greeted Mary and Joseph when they came for the census,* Anne Marie thought. *Nearly two thousand years ago, shepherds were in this field, too, keeping watch over their flocks by night.*

As she stepped from the bus onto the paved square, a swarm of young vendors rushed at her, peddling olive wood bells, postcards, tour books, and other souvenirs.

"No, thank you! No, thank you!" she said, pressing past them and through the crowd in front of the Church of the Nativity.

Anne Marie surveyed the discolored, crumbling walls of the church that towered above the square. She'd expected a magnificent church, perhaps a cathedral, but this place topped by steeples with crosses looked more like a battered fortress. Crouching, she entered the low doorway.

The inside of the main church was also a disappointment—dark, smelling strongly of incense. A jumble of votive lamps hung from the ceiling, flickering in the darkness. A hush filled the sanctuary, despite the hundreds of tourists, many kneeling in prayer, and Anne Marie felt a touch of wonder, a surge of reverence.

Slowly the line of solemn pilgrims moved toward a stairway and, at last, she walked with them down the narrow stairs to the place where tradition said Jesus had been born. At last she stood in the cave that had served as the stable, and then before a silver star on the floor where Jesus had lain.

Sputtering lamps reflected on the old gold icons clustered around the sacred spot, and from her memory came: *And she brought forth her firstborn son, and wrapped him in swaddling clothes, and laid him in a manger; because there was no room for them in the inn.*

Sudden tears blurred her vision, and the words sprang from her soul. "Oh, God, if it's real, I want to know. I want to know what I'm supposed to do with the rest of my life. I'm so tired of struggling...so tired of being alone."

She wished a miracle might occur, that perhaps God would even speak, but there was nothing except the sputtering of the lamps and the rustle of other pilgrims waiting to enter.

Reluctantly, Anne Marie left the cave, finding her way back through the main sanctuary, then past the gardens and cloisters until she was outside the ancient walls. The zealous vendors assailed her again, and she bought a dozen small olive wood bells for Christmas tree ornaments, something for remembrance.

Later, the bus drove to a sprawling gift shop high on the hills of Bethlehem. Inside the shop, displays featured books; jewelry; nativity scenes; inlaid mother-of-pearl boxes; wooden, metal, and pottery religious figures; and more.

Quite suddenly, people across the crowded sales room applauded. Someone shouted across to Anne Marie, "It's Beth and Efrem! They're going to be married!"

The others beamed. Even the Nathans smiled.

"Efrem's buying her an engagement ring!" someone exclaimed.

Somehow she'd have to muster up joy for them, Anne Marie told herself. When Jon glanced in her direction, she quickly looked out to the shepherds' hills.

Far too soon, their group hurried out to the buses. They rode through the hillsides, then back to the outskirts of the bustling city of Jerusalem.

At the elegant King David Hotel, people spoke in excited but hushed tones in the entry. A bomb had blown up a local bus, but the police had the culprits.

There are dangers in the world. I'm concerned about your eternal soul... Aunt Sylvia had said.

Anne Marie tried to forget her aunt's words, tried to avoid Jon, Beth, and Efrem. At any rate, everyone was congratulating the newly engaged couple, and Jon hadn't spotted her. Their group rushed through lunch; it seemed there was never sufficient time to see everything.

Back on the bus, they returned to Jerusalem. Arriving in the city, they went unheeded by the bustling crowds: soldiers with machine guns slung over their shoulders, housewives with loose-mesh grocery bags, colorful merchants at the shops, office workers striding down the sidewalks—Arabs and Jews all together, hurrying about on their business.

The bus stopped to drop them off near the ancient city walls at the Dung Gate, and Efrem gathered his group together before they entered the old city.

"King David made this his capital," he said, "and Solomon built the temple for God. From that time on, Jerusalem has been the holy city for the Jews, and later for the Christians and Muslims."

Anne Marie felt someone staring at her and, looking up, saw Jon. Surely he was wondering about her and Alex again. Humiliated, she glanced away.

"In the middle of the first century before Christ," Efrem continued, "Herod the Great repaired Jerusalem and undertook new building work, including a magnificent new temple. It was to this temple that Jesus' mother brought him as a baby. His parents brought him again when he was twelve to attend Passover. And when he grew up, Jesus regularly visited Jerusalem for religious festivals and to teach and to heal. His arrest, trial, crucifixion, and resurrection all took place in Jerusalem. And several weeks later, on the Day of Pentecost, the Holy Spirit made new people of his followers."

What did that mean "to make new people of Jesus' followers"? Anne Marie wondered. She recalled something about new Christians being new creatures, then dimly: *If any man be in Christ, he is a new creature: old things are passed away; behold, all things are become new.* Amazing how the Sunday school verses she'd memorized came back to her now.

Entering the ancient walled city of Jerusalem, it was as if they had stepped back through the centuries. Here and there palm trees rose at the edge of paved squares of ruins and the old buildings. What had looked like a white-washed city on the hill from the distance now looked musty and crumbled.

At the old temple area, crowds pushed toward the mammoth blocks of the Wailing Wall, the men on their side wearing skull caps, the women on their side in tears as they touched this remnant of Herod's ancient temple. Seeing them, Anne Marie's heart reached out with them in anguish, but hers was for the end of her dream with Alex, for her own loneliness.

With Efrem and the group, she climbed the nearby stone stairway to the city's higher level. To one side, an archaeological dig was underway and a sign pointed to the level upon which Jesus had walked. Beyond was the Dome of the Rock—a seventh-century mosque still under Muslim control. The mosque stood on or near the site where the great Jewish temple had once glistened in the sunshine.

"Jesus taught here," Efrem explained. "Later, the apostle Paul studied here. And it's here that Muslims believe Mohammed sprang to heaven on his horse."

They hurried on and, in the distance, saw the Mount of Olives. "Jesus, riding a white donkey, came to fulfill his destiny here," Efrem said. "An enormous crowd lined the way, calling out and waving palm fronds as he rode down the Mount of Olives toward the Golden Gate leading to the temple. But Jesus saw beyond the triumphant procession, and nearing the city, he wept over it."

Anne Marie followed along with the others. So much sadness and now the unhappiest of all, the *Via Dolorosa.*

"The Way of Sorrows," Efrem explained. "It was here that Jesus, his body broken and bloody, carried the cross."

The group moved slowly through the narrow streets where Jesus had walked, and Anne Marie only felt sadder. In the gloomy Church of the Holy Sepulcher, they viewed the spot where some thought Christ's tomb had been. Tears poured down foreign pilgrims' faces.

Anne Marie found herself filled with even more despair. What had she expected of Jerusalem? Certainly not such sorrow.

As they moved on again through the Via Dolorosa, other tourists dashed into the shops, but she had no heart for shopping, and the smell of cooking sausages and lamb nearly turned her stomach.

Finally, they went to the Garden Tomb and sat down on rows of benches by the ancient white stone walls. Anne Marie sat in despair, slightly away from the others.

First, their guide spoke about the Garden Tomb. "Although some say that the Church of the Holy Sepulcher was Christ's burial place, this was a Jewish cemetery two thousand years ago when Jesus lived as a man on earth. It was a place where people were buried, so it is entirely possible..."

Anne Marie felt even more dismayed. Now a controversy among scholars—and it was already difficult to believe.

When the guide finished, Efrem spoke. "This is where it is said that God raised Christ from the dead...Where God was victorious over evil...Where the battle between good and evil was won! God's victory over evil through Christ is what gives us the hope of eternal life."

When Anne Marie filed by with the others to look into the empty tomb, there was nothing to see but stone walls. The tomb was as empty as her soul.

The sun already had sunk low in the sky when they left the ancient walled city by the Jaffa Gate, where the buses waited to meet them. On the bus, everyone seemed exhausted from the long day. Quiet. Subdued.

Darkness had fallen when they returned to the *Golden Isle* in Haifa. Anne Marie skipped dinner and climbed into bed despondently. She was so tired and despairing that she wished she'd never made the trip, that she'd never come here or seen Alex or Jon again.

As she drifted off into sleep, the meanings of her name came to mind: Anne meant *full of mercy, grace, and prayer;* Marie, *full of bitterness.*

She felt like a Marie.

The next morning on the bus ride to the Sea of Galilee, she tried to rise above her depression. Alone again in a double seat, she gazed out at corn and cotton fields, feeling as lonely as before she'd left home. Worse, it was her own fault; Beth had urged her to ride the other bus with them.

In a matter of days she would be back at Aunt Sylvia's house having to make decisions, Anne Marie thought. What to do with the house...what to do with the rest of her life. Teaching kindergartners was fine for now, but beyond that, life seemed a bleak prospect.

From the front of the bus, the tour guide asked, "Do you see the sheep following the shepherd? Actually following him? It is still the same, much like it was during biblical days."

Anne Marie tried to focus on the sheep in the patchwork of green-and-brown fields and on the occasional villages, but the pastoral views didn't help her heartache.

After a while, the bright blue Sea of Galilee shone in the distance. It was isolated in the countryside, fronted on one side by the small city of Tiberius which dated to Roman days. For a long time, the buses drove along the curving sea, then pulled into a parking lot near the ruins of Capernaum. A sign proclaimed, *The Town of Jesus.*

When they climbed out of the two buses, Efrem gathered his pilgrims around him. "Here Jesus preached in the synagogue, taught by the sea, and healed in the homes. But many who came to watch and to listen did not believe."

Anne Marie glanced up and saw Jon watching her again. As she hurried away after Efrem and the group, she wondered if Jon ever remembered their kiss.

"A mile south of where we walk," Efrem began, "Jesus multiplied the loaves and fishes. Here by the Sea of Galilee, he saw Simon Peter and his brother, Andrew, and said to them, 'Follow me, and I will make you fishers of men.'"

She was surprised to find tears welling in her eyes. How could she feel so miserable here? What was wrong with her? Grabbing a deep breath, she hurried on ahead of the others to the ruins of Capernaum.

Inside the entry, she tried to concentrate on the archaeological site under the trees but found herself peering at the ruins blindly. Nothing gave her comfort. She snapped pictures of the carved remnants of the ancient synagogue, hoping that someday, in a better frame of mind, she might at least enjoy the pictures.

Returning to the bus, she found Jon waiting for her. "Won't you ride with us again, Anne Marie?"

"No, thank you," she replied, then hurried away, near tears. She didn't care for his or anyone else's sympathy over Alex. She wanted to avoid thinking about it, to bury the misery that had her clenching her jaws and fists.

It was only a short bus ride to the green grassy hillside where they would have the worship service. Getting off the bus last, she trailed behind the others on the dusty path. At the path's end, Efrem stood smiling and handed her a program. "I'm afraid you'll have to find a rock for your pew."

"Thanks." She took the program and wandered out to the hillside with the others from Santa Rosita, then found a large flat rock away from the others.

Down below, the blue sea was encircled by rolling foothills, and not too far away, another shepherd led his flock of sheep. The scene was as it must have been when Jesus spoke here to his disciples, she mused. Or had he really? Had he actually existed?

Settling down on the rock, she glanced at the program. On its cover was a picture of this hillside, the "Mount of Beatitudes," where they now sat.

Efrem had already begun the service in the late morning sunshine, his powerful voice easily heard over the warm wind. "When his disciples asked how they should pray to God, Jesus told them." He paused and everyone joined in.

"Our Father which art in heaven," Anne Marie began with them and the familiar words came by rote. What good could they do? Yesterday morning she'd prayed so fervently in Bethlehem in the grotto where Jesus' manger had supposedly been. She'd asked God to dispel her doubts, to help her understand her purpose on earth. Nothing had come of her prayer. Nothing.

The others prayed on, "Thy kingdom come…"

Why was it that her prayers didn't connect? She'd tried to believe in God as a child, too. She'd said nighttime prayers then but had seen no special evidence of God.

Did you ever give your life to Jesus? something from her childhood memories inquired. *Did you give your life to Jesus?*

No, she remembered. She never had. She'd always held

back, always been too stubborn to surrender.

It's not too late, the inner voice said.

A hush seemed to fall over the earth.

God asks you to accept his Son as your Savior and Lord. Say that you'll surrender your life to Jesus.

No! a strident voice argued. *Never! This is all a delusion. It's foolishness!*

She thought of the man traveling to Damascus to persecute the Christians who became converted from Saul, the persecutor, to Paul, the apostle. As a brilliant rabbi, he'd believed in God, but never that Jesus was the Messiah.

A light from heaven, a light brighter than the sun, had shone on him, blinding him, and Jesus had said, "I am Jesus, the one you are persecuting! Now get up and go into the city and await my further instructions."

If it is true, God, Anne Marie prayed, *give me a way to believe! I surrender. I truly surrender."*

When she opened her eyes, peace flooded through her, a peace beyond any she'd ever known. Was this the peace she'd heard about? The peace that passed all understanding?

As she looked out upon the scene, the Sea of Galilee and the foothills and valleys took on an exquisite luminescence. It was as if God was present, surrounding her with his love, burning it into her soul until she, too, seemed to shimmer. Surely she would die of joy and wonder if this ecstasy continued, she thought, but it didn't matter. God's love had touched her.

I believe! she thought. *I do believe!*

In the radiance, time seemed suspended until she heard the others praying, "And forgive us our debts, as we forgive our debtors..."

That meant she had to forgive Alex, to forgive his false assumptions about her, to forgive his leading her on. Forcing herself, she prayed, *I forgive him...and I forgive Lila, no matter what her role in his life might be.* The words were no more out then somehow things began to seem different.

"For thine is the kingdom—

"And the power—

"And the glory, for ever—

"Amen," she breathed with them.

As she opened her eyes, she realized it wasn't Alex or Jon or another man she needed to fill that inner loneliness.

It was Jesus. Quite suddenly it no longer mattered if she had an earthly man to love.

Efrem read from his Bible, "Ye are the light of the world...," and Anne Marie knew where the light had come from. He began to read the Beatitudes, and for the first time, they truly made sense to her.

When Efrem finished, she glanced out across the hillside and found Jon watching her again. She sensed that he—and perhaps others—had been praying for her. Instead of turning, she smiled straight at him, overflowing with joy.

Jon beamed at her in return.

When the service ended, she didn't want to leave. Raising her camera, she took picture after picture of the hillsides and the Sea of Galilee. Here Jesus had walked on the water, just as she had walked forward in faith. Here Jesus had taught his disciples. And here he had filled her with overwhelming joy.

"Anne Marie?" Jon said from behind her.

When she turned, he said, "You look so beautiful."

"You've been praying for me..."

He nodded. "God gave me such peace about you today that I thought something wonderful might happen, and that sunlit smile you sent me was part of it. You looked surprised by joy...overwhelmed by it."

"I am!" Yet it was more than the wonder of faith and joy, it was being whole—for once in her life, being deeply fulfilled.

"That's why Aunt Sylvia wanted me on this trip, isn't it?"

He nodded again. "She told me not to come home for her memorial service under any circumstances—not to help you with estate matters. And she made me promise not to give an explanation until either you came to Christ or the tour ended. It was her last request."

"But why?"

"Your Aunt Sylvia not only spoke to God, she listened."

Anne Marie looked at the shining Sea of Galilee. "God wanted me here. He wanted me here now! I understand. I finally understand!"

On the bus, Anne Marie thought her joy must be evident, but others looked as if their hearts had been touched, too. A reverent silence prevailed. Joyously sitting beside Jon, no words to be spoken.

As the bus drove off, she remembered Aunt Sylvia saying the angels rejoiced over one repentant person. Her aunt must be with them rejoicing!

At the town of Tiberius, they stopped at a rustic seaside restaurant. "St. Peter's fish is the famous dish here," Efrem told them. "It's apparently the same species that was caught here by Peter and the other fishermen two thousand years ago."

Anne Marie decided not to tell the others of her surrender to God. Not yet. Right now, it was enough that Jon knew. He looked blissful, too.

They joined Beth and Efrem at an outdoor table with benches, pretending nothing momentous had happened. With the others they discussed the scenery, and scooped up falafel with bits of pita bread. Next came a salad, and finally the delicious St. Peter's fish. *A dream,* Anne Marie thought. *This feels like a beautiful dream.*

When they finished supper, Jon asked her, "Would you like a walk? Stretch our legs before we get back on the bus? There's a nice breeze."

She nodded and forced herself to get up from the table slowly. God had arranged this, she thought. He had arranged this day and this moment; he had arranged their very lives.

As she and Jon made their way beyond the restaurant toward the water, he reached for her hand and she gladly gave it. Holding hands and striding along, they walked some distance along the Sea of Galilee.

After a time, Jon turned and his eyes met hers. For a moment, neither of them spoke.

Then he touched her face with his fingertips. "You are so precious to me." His gaze lovingly embraced her. "I've known for sure since the moment I woke up on the plane and saw you." He smiled into her eyes.

"You've known—?"

His voice was husky as he continued. "That I love you." He swallowed hard. "I love you."

She caught her breath. "It's been you all this time. I was just too stubborn..."

He touched her lips. And his eyes—as blue as the Sea of Galilee—never left hers. He drew her closer. "I believe God brought us together in his perfect time."

"Oh, Jon, I believe it, too." Her voice was tremulous with emotion.

The sea and the sky shimmered around them. Jon again took her hands in his. "Will you marry me, Anne Marie?"

She felt tears of joy well in her eyes. "I will," she breathed. "Oh, yes, Jon! I will."

"You've just made me the happiest man alive." He looked about, then gave her a wry smile. "Beth and Efrem and the others are probably watching. Does it bother you that we're in their line of sight?"

She gave a quick look around herself. There was only the shoreline and the sea, no secluded place. She smiled. "Actually, very little."

Laughing softly, he cupped her chin within his hands and tilted her face toward his.

As their lips met, the Sea of Galilee lapped softly beside them, and from the outdoor café came a flutter of cheers.

After that, Anne Marie felt only love and heard only the sea.

Dear Reader,

Voyage began when I went on a Middle Eastern cruise with a church group "in the footsteps of the apostle Paul." Although the contemporary characters in the story are fictitious, the settings, trip events, and the historical background are factual.

The first time I visited the island of Patmos—where the apostle John received the Book of Revelation—three of us from our group stopped in the large cave where a monk conveyed in broken English where John listened to God.

Last year, when I revisited the cave in Patmos, it was a Sunday and a Greek Orthodox service was underway. The priest, in gold and white vestments, bobbed rapidly in prayer as have orthodox Jewish worshippers for centuries at the Wailing Wall in Jerusalem—an interesting link of faiths.

God has given me a special desire of my heart. The first time I visited Israel, my husband, an unbeliever, wasn't along, and I wanted so for him to see the wondrous sites with me. On a more recent trip, he came along as a believer. On the Mount of Beatitudes, he was asked to read the Beatitudes. Joy, joy—what tears of joy! As if that weren't joyous enough, we were baptized in the Jordan River.

I wrote *Voyage* for every woman who has ever wanted to go on a holy land pilgrimage and for those who want to relive the wonder of it. I hope it was very real for you.

Love and blessings,

Elaine L. Schulte

Elaine L. Schulte
c/o Palisades
P.O. Box 1720
Sisters, Oregon 97759

PALISADES...PURE ROMANCE

PALISADES

Reunion, Karen Ball
Refuge, Lisa Tawn Bergren
Torchlight, Lisa Tawn Bergren
Treasure, Lisa Tawn Bergren
Chosen, Lisa Tawn Bergren
Firestorm, Lisa Tawn Bergren (October, 1996)
Cherish, Constance Colson
Angel Valley, Peggy Darty
Seascape, Peggy Darty
Sundance, Peggy Darty
Love Song, Sharon Gillenwater
Antiques, Sharon Gillenwater
Secrets, Robin Jones Gunn
Whispers, Robin Jones Gunn
Echoes, Robin Jones Gunn
Coming Home, Barbara Jean Hicks
Glory, Marilyn Kok
Sierra, Shari MacDonald
Forget-Me-Not, Shari MacDonald
Diamonds, Shari MacDonald (November, 1996)
Westward, Amanda MacLean
Stonehaven, Amanda MacLean
Everlasting, Amanda MacLean
Betrayed, Lorena McCourtney
Escape, Lorena McCourtney (September, 1996)
Voyage, Elaine Schulte

A Christmas Joy, Darty, Gillenwater, MacLean
Mistletoe, Ball, Hicks, McCourtney (October, 1996)